The Age
of Asphalt

D1004787

Richard O. Davies

Northern Arizona University

The America's Alternatives Series
Edited by **Harold M. Hyman**

The Age of Asphalt:
The Automobile, the Freeway, and the Condition of Metropolitan America

J.B. Lippincott Company
Philadelphia/New York /Toronto

Tennessee Tech Library
Cookeville, TN

Copyright © 1975 by J. B. Lippincott Company. All rights reserved.

This book is fully protected by copyright, and, with the exception of brief extracts for review, no part of it may be reproduced in any form, by print, photoprint, microfilm, or any other means, without written permission of the publisher.

ISBN 0-397-47327-3
Library of Congress Catalog Card Number 74-31055
Printed in the United States of America

1 3 5 7 9 8 6 4 2

Library of Congress Cataloging in Publication Data

Davies, Richard O.
    The age of asphalt.

    (The America's alternatives series)
    Bibliography: p.
    1. Transportation, Automotive—United States.
2. Urban transportation—United States. 3. Automobiles—
Social aspects—United States. I. Title.
HE5623.D27   388.4'1'0973   74-31055
ISBN 0-397-47327-3

This book is dedicated,
with
happy memories, to my 1953 Chevy.
May it rest in peace.

Contents

Foreword

"When you judge decisions, you have to judge them in the light of what there was available to do it," noted Secretary of State George C. Marshall to the Senate Committees on the Armed Services and Foreign Relations in May 1951.[1] In this spirit, each volume in the "America's Alternatives" series examines the past for insights which History—perhaps only History—is peculiarly fitted to offer. In each volume the author seeks to learn why decision-makers in crucial public policy or, more rarely, private choice situations adopted a course and rejected others. Within this context of choices, the author may ask what influence then-existing expert opinion, administrative structures, and budgetary factors exerted in shaping decisions? What weights did constitutions or traditions have? What did men hope for or fear? On what information did they base their decisions? Once a decision was made, how was the decision-maker able to enforce it? What attitudes prevailed toward nationality, race, region, religion, or sex, and how did these attitudes modify results?

We freely ask such questions of the events of our time. This "America's Alternatives" volume transfers appropriate versions of such queries to the past.

In examining those elements that were a part of a crucial historical decision, the author has refrained from making judgments based upon attitudes, information, or values that were not current at the time the decision was made. Instead, as much as possible he or she has explored the past in terms of data and prejudices known to persons contemporary to the event.

---

[1] U.S. Congress, Senate, Hearings Before the Committees on the Armed Services and the Foreign Relations of the United States, *The Military Situation in the Far East*, 82 Cong., 2d sess., part I, p. 382. Professor Ernest R. May's "Alternatives" volume directed me to this source and quotation.

Nevertheless, the following reconstruction of one of America's major alternative choices speaks implicitly and frequently, explicitly to present concerns.

In form, this volume consists of a narrative and analytical historical essay (Part One), within which the author has identified by use of headnotes (i.e., Alternative 1, etc.) the choices which he believes were actually before the decision-makers with whom he is concerned.

Part Two of this volume contains, in whole or part, the most appropriate source documents that illustrate the Part One Alternatives. The Part Two Documents and Part One essay are keyed for convenient use (i.e., references in Part One will direct readers to appropriate Part Two Documents). The volume's Part Three offers users further guidance in the form of a Bibliographic Essay.

For tens of millions of Americans, gasoline shortages during the energy crunch that began in 1973 raised for the first time since the automobile's emergence fifty years ago as the nation's primary people mover, questions about its benefits and costs. In this volume, Dean Richard O. Davies of Northern Arizona University's College of Public and Environmental Service, recreates the situation resulting in the decision during President Eisenhower's administration in favor of the interstate highway system. It is almost forgotten that alternatives existed then that could have made us far less dependent on the automobile and, as events developed, to the vagaries of international oil diplomacy and politics. Dean Davies's careful analysis and revealing supportive documents offer opportunity to reconstruct that choice situation, now so meaningful.

Harold M. Hyman
Rice University

Preface

The essay that follows is an intensely personal interpretation of an extraordinarily complex sequence of events that produced our contemporary urban transportation crisis. The pressing need for improved urban transit systems is acknowledged today by virtually everyone concerned with the future of our cities. Yet, as will become clear in the following pages, such was not always the case. One cannot understand the contemporary "energy crisis" or the much larger and more complex "urban crisis" without the long view afforded by history. When the nation opted for the freeway system as the means of meeting urban transportation needs during the mid-fifties, few Americans thought in terms of possible exhaustion of energy sources, or even about environmental impact. Those were days which in retrospect seem much more innocent and less complicated than life in the mid-seventies.

My harsh treatment of the Eisenhower administration, I feel, is justified by subsequent events. The administration did blunder because, as the early parts of the narrative indicate, it inherited a *modus operandi* that virtually dictated the solution that was adopted. The shortsighted leadership of the nation during the 1950s, I am certain, will shock many of the college-age readers who manage to conquer the pages that follow. Yet this attitude of the administration, as expressed in the formulation of the highway policy that resulted, was typical of those complacent years that I often refer to in my classroom lectures as the "Eisenhower Equilibrium." After all, these were the golden and now nostalgic days of Elvis, rock'n roll, tail fins on automobiles, duck-cut hair, leather jackets on motorcycle fiends, and hoola hoops. These were, I must confess, my own innocent and uncomplicated college years. And, reasonably concerned about national affairs as I was, I cannot even recall the passage of the important legislation that is central to this book!

It is my sincere hope that the narrative that follows will provide the reader with a reasonably accurate understanding of how decisions are often made in our democracy. Reasonable alternatives, he may observe, are sometimes overlooked or ignored; the heavy weight of tradition and precedent, the powerful clout of special interests, the pristine faith in public opinion, somehow coalesce into reluctant sputterings from Congress. Such was the case of the birth of our freeway system. To the policy makers during the mid-fifties, the pressing problems that demanded early solution were jammed city streets, overcrowded two-lane highways, and the need to move more and more automobiles ever more quickly. But twenty years later, the priorities have shifted drastically. Now the American people, and hence their elected officials, ponder the dilemmas of gasoline shortages and the fragile condition of our environment. Thus does one's view change with the passing of time.

Finally, in view of several critical comments contained herein about the American obsession for the automobile, a confession is in order. I own today, two gasoline-gobbling vehicles: a traditional American sedan, vintage 1971, that is virtually indispensable for the daily functioning of my active family; and an antiquated four-wheeler with which I would part only upon pain of death . . . for it holds the key to my infrequent escapes from the ravages of daily life into the backwoods of Arizona's incomparable and still primitive mountains where I can rest, relax, think great thoughts, and occasionally outguess a two-pound trout.

No study such as this can be accomplished without the assistance of many persons. I especially wish to acknowledge the assistance of the staff at the Dwight D. Eisenhower Library and its able director, Dr. John Wickman. Additional research for this volume was done under a summer grant from the Harry S. Truman Institute, which made possible a visit to the National Archives in Washington, D.C. Dr. Mark Rose, whose knowledge of American highway politics far exceeds my own, provided invaluable suggestions. Without the support and encouragement of the general editor of this series, Professor Harold Hyman, this book would never have been completed. Special acknowledgments are due my colleague, Joseph M. Ferguson, Jr., who shared with me the benefit of his facile command of the subtleties of our language, and Mrs. Thelma Hazlett and Mrs. Margaret Arnold, who courageously worked their way through the illegible maze of my amateurish typing and illegible scrawl to produce a readable manuscript. Further, to Jenny and Bobby, I extend a fatherly hug for their patience and their understanding of why I could not always go to a movie or toss a football. And finally, a special public word of "thanks" once more to that wonderful girl who understands, never complains and somehow perseveres . . . my lovely wife Sharon.

Richard O. Davies
Northern Arizona University

Part One

The Age of Asphalt

1

Freeways or Mass Transit

The sun shone brightly in Los Angeles that fateful day of December 30, 1940. The governor of California, Culbert Olson, was there to snip the ribbon, while Rose Bowl Queen Sally Stanton and her court were on hand to lend glamour to the ceremonies. After more than two years of construction, the first freeway in Los Angeles was to be opened; the Arroyo Seco, later renamed the Pasadena Freeway, had already been dubbed "the miracle bouleyard" by an enthusiastic public. Governor Olson praised the promoters of the freeway, observing that "it takes courage to do a thing the first time." And as high school bands blared and balloons drifted upward into the crystal-clear blue winter sky, the smiling governor snipped the ribbon and four hundred anxious drivers moved their automobiles down the shiny new ribbon of concrete. The City of the Angels moved bravely into the era of the freeway.

Little did onlookers realize the far-reaching significance of the simple ceremony they witnessed. This six-mile stretch of freeway would set the mold for the development of urban transportation in the United States for the next half-century or more. It is now increasingly evident that an overreliance upon the automobile as the primary means of intraurban travel, as encouraged by federal assistance to freeway and related street development, was an unfortunate mistake. However, at the time that important decisions were made, it did not seem so; in fact, it has been only with the passage of time that new problems emerged, thereby creating new perspectives upon the relationship of man to the automobile within an urban context. An examination of the making of the decisions that produced an imbalanced urban transportation system based on the private automobile is illuminating for those who are currently seeking new solutions in mass transit. Yet, as will be seen, many enormous difficulties also exist in that field, and they in turn are related to the importance of the automobile within the broad context of "the American way of life." It is readily apparent that Americans still prefer the alternative of the automobile to mass transit, and that preference lies deeply rooted in the past three-quarters of a century of American history.

Original Hopes and Emerging Flaws

During the fifteen years after World War II, the "freeway" concept, featuring multilane, limited-access thoroughfares providing relatively safe high-speed highways, gained enormous public support. Nearly everyone got on the freeway bandwagon, especially state and federal highway officials; trucking interests, road builders, politicians and, most importantly, the millions of automobile owners. By the mid-fifties, it seemed, no public figure of importance opposed their construction either as links between cities in a new national highway network, or for commuter travel within cities.

As a result of massive public support for safer and faster highways and demands for an end to traffic congestion on city streets, Congress created the National System of Interstate and Defense Highways in 1956 (Alternative 1: see Document 2). This system was to be financed by funds derived from a new Highway Trust Fund and would lace the nation with forty-one thousand miles of freeways, including seven thousand miles within metropolitan areas. Nearly all cities of populations in excess of fifty thousand would be included in the system. Original plans called for the completion of the system in 1972 at a total cost of about $26 billion. In 1968 Congress added an additional fifteen hundred miles to the system, and changes in engineering specifications, political complicity, and administrative problems pushed the completion date into the early 1980s. Rising labor and materials costs would ultimately push the construction costs near the $100 billion mark.

Virtually no one challenged the system when it was established. Congress uncritically accepted the questionable claims by the Eisenhower administration and its many boosters that the system was essential for national defense—for the evacuation of cities in the event of atomic attack, and the rapid movement of troops and equipment in time of national emergency. Even in the heyday of Republican fiscal conservatism few dared challenge the enormous costs of the program, despite the fact that it would be the biggest and most expensive public works project in history; the much-maligned expenditures of Franklin Roosevelt's entire New Deal paled in comparison. No less an authority than the archconservative Secretary of the Treasury George M. Humphrey gave it his fiscal blessing: "America lives on wheels, and we have to provide the highways to keep America living on wheels and keep the kind and form of life we want."[1]

Enthusiasm soared. One national highway network with high standards of engineering efficiency and the latest concepts of highway construction and safety design would cut the appalling incidence of highway fatalities and eliminate ' time-consuming and irritating delays on overcrowded and truck-congested two-lane highways. City planners hailed the new system as a means of uniting the city by making it possible for suburban residents to commute swiftly to their jobs in the central business district; furthermore, the highways would blend neatly into the planners' ambitious plans for slum clearance and urban renewal in the blighted areas of the central city. Local politicos, hard pressed to pay the rapidly rising costs of government, joyously received the financing formula that would have the federal government paying ninety percent of the urban freeway costs, leaving the state government the remainder! It is not every day that a financially troubled city can get a spanking-new transportation system virtually for free.

As could be expected, road builders and contractors were beside themselves with joy. The days of bonanza had arrived. Oil company executives joined in the celebration, as did the nation's automobile manufacturers, because the Interstate system meant that the national policy for decades ahead was set—the private automobile and the truck transport were to provide the great bulk of the nation's transportation requirements, moving both people and goods. And President Eisenhower and his administration were equally pleased: they had launched the greatest construction project in the history of mankind since the building of the Great Wall of China and the construction of the Roman Highway.

The euphoria of 1956 would not last. Originally hailed by nearly all Americans as a rational and effective solution to the nation's complex transportation needs, the Interstate system, especially its heavily traveled urban segments, would come under increasingly heavy criticism during the sixties and seventies. It would sharply divide urban planners as well as government officials. It would generate angry citizen protest movements. Its heavy contribution to urban noise and air pollution would evoke intense criticism, and the devastating impact it had upon the neighborhoods which it crossed would produce intense reactions. The unexpected contributions it made to increased traffic congestion, and its severe economic impact upon the central business district would spark additional angry criticism. The aesthetic-minded would assail the destruction of famous buildings and historical landmarks, while environmentalists would decry the tendency of efficiency-minded highway engineers to cut huge swaths through valuable parks or the few remaining wooded areas in a city. The manner in which the expressway rapidly accelerated metropolitan sprawl would produce severe criticisms from urban experts. And during the gasoline shortage of the mid-seventies, energy experts and city planners would agree that the most shortsighted of all aspects of the Interstate concept was that it undercut the nation's railroads as a means of moving both goods and people medium and long distances, and that it had a devastating impact upon existing urban transit systems. Even more seriously, it prevented the development of these systems during the important years of the 1960s. In sum, critics charged that the urban segment of the Interstate system shut off many avenues for diversification of the nation's transportation system at a critical time and forced upon American society an essentially one-dimensional transportation system based on the truck and automobile that assumed unlimited supplies of fuel for the foreseeable future.

Framework of the Decision

A careful study of the process of making the vital decision which would produce the Interstate system and shape American society for decades to come is a shocking revelation of the uncritical and unimaginative attitude of those involved. The Eisenhower administration made its decision within a very narrow framework, which did not provide for a consideration of viable alternatives. No effort was made to challenge naive assumptions of highway experts or the selfish interests of the Highway Lobby; no serious considerations of a companion program to aid urban mass transit systems were included in the highway program. The potential—and later proven—calamitous impact upon the nation's railroads received scant attention. No concern for existing commuter trains or bus systems was evidenced. The records of the Eisenhower administration and other political leaders and special interest groups reveal that those in a position of power and responsibility actually had no understanding of the probable consequences of their actions. And, it is further evident that they did not even want to learn what the consequences might be.

The inescapable conclusion is that the Eisenhower administration determined that the nation—including the metropolitan areas—needed a new network of multilane highways. It made no serious effort to consider the implications that the system held for the future of the cities of the nation; equally important, it did not *even want* to consider available alternatives.

Thus it was not until the consequences of the Interstate system were widely recognized that important public dialogue began on possible alternatives. It was not until more than two-thirds of the entire system had been built that the efforts of citizens' groups, urban experts, and social critics succeeded in focusing attention upon the inherent weaknesses of the urban segment of the Interstate and opened up discussion of mass transit alternatives. By that time it was already much too late. Unless a powerful countermovement could be generated in the 1970s under the intense pressures of a possibly prolonged energy crisis, the 1956 National Highway Aid Act, with the overwhelming lever of billions of dollars for getting additional highway construction, had frozen the nation's alternative transportation systems. Six thousand miles of urban freeways had been built and an additional one thousand miles were under construction or in the planning stage. The Highway Trust Fund, with its billions of dollars, had created a powerful momentum of its own, and the Highway Lobby remained one of the most powerful pressure groups in the nation. The structure of metropolitan America had been sculptured by an automobile-inspired, haphazard, and unplanned sprawl; the nation found itself tied to an imbalanced and irrational transportation system that was not only wasteful of precious energy sources, but destructive to the quality of life in its metropolitan centers as well.

By failing carefully to examine the assumptions upon which the Interstate system was based, and by failing to probe the implications of that system, the decision makers during the mid-fifties were derelict in their responsibilities. By refusing to consider available alternatives, and by accepting the unchallenged importance of the automobile, they placed upon future American generations heavy burdens, both financial and social.

The decision to build the Interstate system, however, should not be viewed as merely the result of shortsighted leadership from members of the Eisenhower administration. To be sure, Dwight D. Eisenhower fervently wanted the program because it would alleviate a pressing political problem in the face of the 1956 presidential campaign: at the time, it did seem to contain the logical solution to the spiralling traffic accident rates and growing urban rush hour traffic jams. Beyond these immediate concerns, however, it would also fulfill a lifelong dream that the president had held ever since that miserable time when he had slogged his way through the spring mud of Kansas on a coast-to-coast army maneuver in 1921. In the mid-fifties, when Soviet-American relationships were bogged down in the bitterest years of the Cold War, the rationale of national defense perhaps had merit: The Interstate would facilitate the rapid movement of troops and equipment. And, should an atomic attack occur, freeways would supposedly facilitate urban evacuation.

Actually the "decision" by the Eisenhower administration merely put into action a program that had been designed by highway officials before World War II and approved by the Franklin D. Roosevelt administration; had it not been for the knotty problems of postwar inflation and the semi-war in Korea, the Interstate concept probably would have been launched by the Truman administration. Retreating further into the past in search of origins, the Interstate system can be seen to have evolved out of the approach to road construction first implemented during the administration of Woodrow Wilson with the Federal Aid Highway Act of 1916. This law created the concept of a federal highway network and had received endorsement and increased funding from each succeeding administration. It can be said with a great deal of accuracy that by the mid-fifties conditions had finally become right for the establishment of the immense Interstate system: heavy urban growth, increased use of the automobile, much publicized traffic fatalities, rush hour congestion, overcrowded and antiquated two-lane intercity highways, and, especially, mounting public demands for action to end these problems.

The Automobile in the "American Dream"

Ever since its introduction at the turn of the century, the American people have been hopelessly in love with the automobile. It not only provided greater freedom and mobility, but also appealed to the American fascination for power and technology. The automobile and its big cousin, the heavy-duty transport truck, provided for rapid travel between farm and city. The automobile also freed the urban American from the clutches of trolley schedules. In effect, the automobile constituted a personalized urban mass transit system, allowing the owner to travel about the city whenever or wherever he desired.

When Henry Ford received a portentous $28,000 loan from a Detroit bank in 1903 to launch the Ford Motor Company, there were less than 10,000 automobiles in the United States—a ratio of about 9,500 persons per auto. By the early 1970s, however, that ratio had been reduced to one auto for every two persons; 3,200,000 Americans were born, but American automobile manufacturers produced twice that number of automobiles.

The automobile not only provided reasonable, reliable transportation, but also became part of the important imagery and symbolism that affects American daily life. The make, model, and style of an automobile serve as an expression of its owner's status as well as a reflection of his value system. The American people quickly saw in the automobile a new freedom and mobility. As Winthrop Scarrett wrote in "The Horse of the Future and the Future of the Horse," an essay in *Harper's Weekly* in 1907, "In the last analysis the automobile means that man has finally segregated a little bit of the giant forces of nature and hitched it to his individual chariot. What human mind can measure the meaning of this mighty fact? The automobile is to become the ready, tireless and faithful servant of man throughout the world where civilization has a home or freedom a banner." And in a prophecy of unerring accuracy, Scarrett observed, "Yesterday it was the plaything of the few, today it is the servant of many, tomorrow it will be the necessity of humanity."

During the 1920s—that supposed decade of "normalcy" and conservatism which nonetheless produced far-reaching changes in American life—the American people assimilated the automobile into their life style. Woodrow Wilson had become the first president to ride to his inauguration in a vehicle propelled by an internal combustion engine; yet the horse still provided the primary means of transportation during the First World War. Even as the nation was selecting Warren G. Harding as its next president, the automobile remained largely an expensive toy, still an unproved curiosity. By 1930, however, twenty-six million automobiles were registered in the United States. No longer an object of curiosity and a plaything of the rich, the automobile had become an integral part of the daily lives of most American families.

As a new symbol of the age of automobility, Henry Ford became a folk-hero in his own time. The American love affair with chromium and powerful engines had become fact. Cities rushed to pave their muddy streets, and state governments appropriated huge sums to hard-top the dusty country roads. Farmers demanded hard-surfaced roads to their markets. Federal funds poured into the forty-eight states on a fifty-fifty matching basis to build essential bridges and to pay for paving. In 1925, the United States Chamber of Commerce, in an effort to encourage road building, praised the automobile because it afforded its owners "the ability to live in pleasant and healthful surroundings yet depend on transportation facilities that permit work in the urban centers." Housing developers opened up new subdivisions on the edges of the cities, and the suburbanization of America received a powerful new impetus. Not surprisingly, Sinclair Lewis made his symbol for the American middle class of the 1920s a real estate developer; his fictional character, George F. Babbitt, offered middle-class families an easy escape from the difficulties of urban living in "Glen Oriole Estates." The automobile constituted the means of that escape from the congestion and racial-ethnic polyglot of the city of Zenith.

The Economics of the Automobile Culture

Following the hiatus imposed by the Great Depression and the Second World War, the automobile culture reached new and dizzy heights, culminating not surprisingly in the most expensive and elaborate public works project in history—the 1956 Highway Aid Act. America had entered the heyday of the Age of Asphalt. During the 1920s Kansas City real estate developer J. C. Nichols had built the nation's first shopping center. The enterprising and imaginative Nichols designed his plaza for the automobile age, and coupled its construction with his exclusive Country Club housing development for the Kansas City monied aristocracy. Whereas the plaza featured lovely Spanish architecture and many sculptures and fountains, imitators during the great period of growth following World War II emphasized stark functionalism that often resulted in an impermanent plastic-neon-prefabricated appearance. The models, of sorts, were the "Bohack" grocery stores in New Jersey, which were planned for customers who would arrive by automobile rather than on foot. This idea was quickly emulated throughout the nation. The garage, and later the open-sided "carport," became the most prominent feature of new houses; the "drive-in" concept was employed profitably by restaurants, outdoor motion picture theatres, liquor stores, and banks. Huge shopping centers appeared on the edges of cities, gobbling up thousands of acres merely for automobile parking. Motel chains, such as the pioneering Holiday Inns of America, erected convenient highway locations, undercutting traditional "tourist homes" or "mom and pop" tourist cabins as well as downtown hotels. And standing on nearly every corner of city thoroughfares was the service station, mute symbol of the importance of the omnipresent automobile within modern American life.

In 1970, the zenith of the Age of Asphalt, Americans drove their automobiles more than one trillion miles and spent over $93 billion to buy, operate, insure, park, and build roads for their automobiles. Between 1955 and 1970, Americans had purchased nearly one hundred million automobiles.

The automobile thus became a vital cog in the national economy. Out of a welter of small and highly competitive enterprises early in the century—Essex, Maxwell, Winton, Studebaker, Olds, LaSalle, Stutz, Chevrolet, Packard, Ford, etc.—there emerged by the late 1920s a concentration of several large manufacturers. By the 1950s the "big three" of General Motors, Chrysler, and Ford dominated automobile markets. The automobile industry accounted for about one-sixth of the Gross National Product, if one includes manufacture, sales, repair, and such subsidiary "spin-off" industries as upholstery, insurance, glass, oil, rubber tires, and electronics. Whenever the nation's economy turned "soft," presidents from Truman through Nixon instinctively turned to devices to stimulate automobile manufacture sales. Thus in 1973, a total of 112,000,000 automobiles were registered in the United States; significantly, each had a life expectancy when new of just five years. And a well-conditioned American people readily accepted the fact of an annual automobile fatality number of over fifty thousand along with four million injured.

Less noticeable, perhaps, but equally important, was the role played by the trucking industry. In 1973 a total of twenty million trucks were registered in the United States and traveled an astronomical number of 500 million ton miles. Trucks traveling the national highways had become the new "life-line" of an advanced postindustrial civilization.

The insatiable infatuation of the American people for the automobile was accompanied by an incessant demand for better roads upon which to drive. As a cursory survey of American history shows, the American people have long been concerned about improved transportation. The National (or Cumberland) Road received enthusiastic acclaim in the 1820s as it opened up the New West for trade. State governments scrambled to build canals and then railroads as the economy expanded during the mid-nineteenth century. The often overlooked popularity of the bicycle prompted considerable demand for paved roads during the late nineteenth century. The arrival of the automobile, however, crystallized the "good roads" movement. In 1910, 468,000 automobiles struggled through the mud and/or dust of city and country roads.

Mounting public pressure produced the Federal Aid Highway Act of 1916, which established the concept of a national highway system. The act authorized the expenditure of $75 million for road construction by 1921, and stipulated that participating states would match each federal dollar received. Further, the states assumed total responsibility for maintenance. The funds, however, could be spent only on rural toll free roads costing less than $10,000 per mile, and the Department of Agriculture was given the responsibility for administration. This was reasonable, in that one of the major objectives was the improvement of farm-to-market roads, primarily for the benefit of the isolated farmer. Although the stated purpose of the new construction program was to get farmers out of the mud, its sponsors also intended that it would promote a national system of connecting trunk highways. High hopes were held for this new program of federal-state cooperation, and the states jumped into action enthusiastically in an effort to improve the nation's 2,455,761 miles of rural roads, of which only 11-1/2 percent were hard-surfaced. During the period 1917-18, some 559 projects covering 6,250 miles and costing $42,300,000 were approved. The war effort virtually halted road construction at that time, but with the Armistice, it resumed with renewed vigor.

The emergency of war had demonstrated that the United States needed a coherent network of trunk highways instead of a fragmented network of farm-to-market roads. During the war, the railroads had been overwhelmed and the growing number of truck transports gave an impressive demonstration of their potential as long distance carriers. Good highways, however, were needed for them to reach this potential.

Heavier vehicles, increased volumes of traffic, and higher speeds posed new problems for highway designers and underscored the need for better roads. Obviously what was needed was a new, comprehensive highway plan, and Congress responded with the Federal Aid Act of 1921. This act created the Federal Aid Highway System, which was to receive all federal money appropriated for highway construction. It was designed to create a coherent highway network by requiring that federal aid be concentrated upon "such projects as will expedite the completion of an adequate and connected system of highways, interstate in character." The states were required to spend all federal aid on a designated system not exceeding seven percent of the total national highway mileage. Not more than three-sevenths of the total designated miles could be primary or interstate highway, while the remainder were to be secondary or intercounty roads. A minimum of sixty percent of the federal aid was to be spent on the primary network. For the first time, the United States would have a national system consisting of approximately two hundred thousand miles of primary and secondary roads.

The twenties were thus understandably boom years for the automobile manufacturers and road builders. Everyone—politicians, contractors, truckers, and motorists—demanded better highways to meet the increasing number of vehicles on the streets and roads. During the 1920s more than seventeen million cars, trucks, and buses were added to the nation's motor fleet, and the number of miles of surfaced highways reached 407,000. Total annual expenditure on roads increased from $1,385,000,000 in 1921 to $2,852,000,000 in 1930. In ten short years, the nation's highway system had advanced from a primitive state to that of the best in the world. By 1930, improved roads had finally caught up with the heavy demands placed upon them.

From Local to National Transport

In the late twenties and early thirties, a number of significant changes occurred in the federal government's policies of highway financing. In 1928, federal funds were authorized for municipalities exceeding twenty-five hundred inhabitants; thus, federal aid was no longer restricted to rural areas, as it had been in the primary system established in 1921. The depression also altered a basic purpose of federal aid from building adequate roads to that of providing economic recovery and relief. In an effort to create work for the unemployed, emergency funds were appropriated in 1933 for expenditure on federal aid highways passing through any municipality, as well as for secondary and feeder roads. Under such conditions, some stipulations such as the fifty-fifty matching funds of the states were temporarily abandoned.

The great need for public works meant that highway improvements were oriented to local needs instead of being pushed forward toward completion of the primary system of federal arterial highways. In 1936, the local nature of road work was incorporated into federal highway policy when a system of secondary feeder roads became eligible for federal aid. The new legislation appropriated $25 million for aiding states to improve secondary roads, "including farm-to-market roads, rural free delivery mail roads, and public-school bus routes." Although the new law did not place a limit on the number of miles in the secondary system, a limit of ten percent of the total road miles in the state was administratively established.

Although the 1930s saw an expansion of the federal aid system into secondary roads and a concentration of expenditures in local areas, the same decade saw the appearance of high-speed, large-volume highways that pointed the way to the future. In New York, Connecticut, Pennsylvania, and California, highway officials moved forward with construction of several parkways and proto-freeways designed for high-speed, long distance travel.

Congressional interest in a national system of "super-highways" was shown in the Federal Aid Act of 1938, which directed the head of the Bureau of Public Roads (BPR) to advise Congress on the feasibility of building six super-highways, three running north-south and three running east-west. Congress also desired information on the feasibility of financing these as toll roads. The BPR report, "Toll Roads and Free Roads," appeared in 1939 and recommended improvement of an interregional network of main transportation arteries. The report considered tolls an inadequate method of finance and, because of the predominantly national importance of such a system, recommended that the federal portion of the costs be increased over that of the regular Federal Aid Highway system. However, planning for this and other possible highway networks, as well as current construction work on all other highways, was interrupted by World War II.

A growing possibility of involvement in World War II led President Roosevelt in 1940 to include highways as part of his administration's plans for a new defense system. He directed the Federal Works Agency and the War Department to make a survey of the highway system as related to defense; the ensuing report recommended a series of improvements on highways related to defense, including upgrading a seventy-five thousand mile system of highways essential for the national defense. Most of the federal roads in the 1939 report were included in the new defense network, and the Defense Highway Act of 1941 attempted to implement several suggestions contained in the report; one important feature of the 1941 bill provided that the federal portion of the cost of the strategic highways be increased to seventy-five percent of the total.

The war effort stopped most highway construction, and shortages of labor and material caused extensive deterioration in existing roads because adequate maintenance was impossible. As had been the case in 1917-18, war once more called attention to the need for more and better highways. The importance of an efficient and reliable highway system to expedite the movement of troops and military equipment had been deeply impressed upon national leaders. This rationale would later be used to justify the Interstate system.

When the BPR began planning for postwar construction, it recognized the importance of a long-range, coordinated highway program. A number of important departures incorporated in the Federal Aid Highway Act of 1944 pointed toward an expanded federal role in future highway development. The first of these new initiatives included a large increase in annual federal appropriations—a total of $1.5 billion for the three fiscal years immediately following the end of the war. Officials believed these appropriations necessary to reconstruct thousands of miles of deteriorating highways and to provide an estimated five million jobs for returning servicemen. In a second major innovation Congress specifically included urban areas in the federal aid program, realizing that while federal aid had helped pull the farmer out of the mud, it had never provided substantial aid for the congested cities. For the first time Congress passed a specific appropriation of $125 million for urban primary roads. The growing need for better roads within urban centers had finally been recognized. Congress thus established what was called the "A-B-C" program, with funds allocated on a matching basis in a ratio of forty-five percent for regular primary roads, thirty percent for the secondary system, and twenty-five percent for urban projects.

In 1941, President Roosevelt created a special Inter-regional Highway Committee to prepare a master plan for postwar highway construction. This final report essentially endorsed the idea of Thomas H. MacDonald, commissioner of the Bureau of Public Roads. The plan called for a highway system that would connect urban centers, thereby facilitating high speed traffic from the downtown area to outlying areas. These urban segments would then be tied to a national expressway system of thirty-four thousand miles. The committee strongly argued that the plan would stop urban decay and would curb decentralization.

In the final section of the Federal Highway Act of 1944, Congress endorsed the recommendations of the president's Inter-regional Highway Committee and approved "in principle" a national system of interstate highways not to exceed forty thousand miles

so located as to connect by routes, as direct as practicable, the principle metropolitan areas, cities, and industrial centers, to serve the national defense, and to connect at suitable border points with routes of continental importance in the Dominion of Canada and the Republic of Mexico.

Although no funds were appropriated nor the ratio of federal aid increased, this provided the framework for the Interstate and Defense Highway System in 1956. Federal highway officials apparently hoped that the states would consider the Interstate system sufficiently important for relief of urban congestion and unemployment to warrant the use of the money allocated for the primary system. However, congressional failure to appropriate special funds or to reduce the state's share of construction costs meant the construction on the Interstate system would not begin for more than a decade. With the states required to pay fifty percent of the construction costs, the superhighways were too expensive at a time when nearly every existing road in America was in serious need of repair or reconstruction. A more generous federal contribution would be required.

The Postwar Highway Crisis

At the end of the Second World War, state and federal highway officials looked optimistically toward the future. They recognized that the additional millions of new vehicles crowding upon the nation's streets and roads each year entailed a bonanza for their programs. Contractors were equally delighted. The $500 million annual federal appropriation to the states, combined with the expected extra effort at the local and state level, would fuel a highway construction boom. However, the highway officials had to deal first with the seriously deteriorated condition of the nation's existing roads. The anticipated new construction also suffered from the problems of "reconversion" from a wartime to a peacetime economy—shortages of equipment and supplies, lengthy labor disputes, and especially inflation. By mid-1946 prices in highway construction had jumped by fifty percent over prewar levels. Meanwhile, the number of motor vehicles increased much faster than anticipated. By 1950 more than forty-nine million vehicles traveled 458 billion miles within the United States, a volume not expected until the late fifties. Thus this huge volume of traffic had to be accommodated by a highway and street system that had been built largely before 1930.

By the early 1950s it had become obvious to everyone that a major highway crisis existed. Nearly every state government authorized research studies to determine their needs. These important technical research reports, however, were structured by state highway officials so that the conclusions of the "independent" consultants would confirm the validity of the programs already planned by the state highway departments (for an exception, see Document 1). As Mark Rose observes in his detailed study of highway policies during the 1950s, "they were supposed to win 'public understanding' for their conclusions and provide important data to government officials attempting to withstand the 'sharpening demands' of the vastly increased number of motor vehicle operators."[2] Rapidly growing traffic volume, intensification of urban congestion, as well as national defense requirements all pressed in on federal and state officials. Consequently, highway officials began to push hard for the creation of an urban expressway construction program to alleviate many of these problems. The federal commissioner of Public Roads, Thomas H. MacDonald proclaimed that the expressways were *the* means of saving the "cities from stagnation and decay." Blithely ignoring mass transit alternatives, he argued that the crucial question facing the cities was, "Shall we build highways which will enable traffic to move into and through the city quickly and safely, or shall be try to get along with things as they are?"[3] MacDonald, it can safely be said, was not a man to betray highway interests with such radical alternatives as subways, commuter trains, or buses.

In 1952, highway officials estimated that over sixty percent of the 660,000 miles of the existing Federal Highway System was inadequate to handle daily load requirements. Safety officials blamed the hefty four percent annual increase in traffic fatalities upon the overcrowded and inadequate highway system. In that year, a Bureau of Public Roads report estimated that a minimum of twenty years of construction at a cost of $40 billion would be necessary to bring the nation's highways up to an acceptable standard.

With highway costs mounting, and with the Truman administration bogged down in Korea and unable to promote a more adequate highway network, many states turned to toll roads as a means of obtaining much-needed superhighways in densely populated areas. The toll charges produced none of the political problems feared by many officials. The great successes of this type of expressway in some twenty states showed that motorists were willing to pay for less congested interregional highways. In the early 1950s the number of miles of toll roads increased rapidly, with more than one thousand miles completed and seven thousand more miles planned by 1955.

Pennsylvania provided the model. Shortly before the war, state leaders had bravely sought to emulate the much acclaimed *Autobahn*, Adolph Hitler's contribution to highway engineering. The Pennsylvania Turnpike, transportation experts concluded, proved to be cheap at twice the cost. Not only did it move traffic more rapidly, but at substantially less operational cost per mile. By 1946 it was carrying a daily traffic load far in excess of the most optimistic predictions. In a situation of intense competition not unlike that between the states when the canal and early railroad systems were developed a century earlier, nearby states moved quickly to emulate Pennsylvania's innovation. The New Jersey Turnpike was authorized in 1948, and the following year Ohio began to plan its own version that would connect with the Indiana Turnpike and thus create a multilane ribbon from Cleveland to Chicago. New York built its "New York Thruway," and Oklahoma and Kansas plunged into the toll road business with the Will Rogers and Kansas turnpikes. The toll road boom, however, stopped abruptly in 1956 with the creation of the Interstate System. Yet during the short time of its existence, it had convinced highway planners that the American people were anxious to have better highways, and that they were willing—even eager—to pay the cost.

Notes

1. Quoted in Mark Howard Rose, "Express Highway Politics, 1939-1956" (Ph.D. dissertation, Ohio State University, 1973), p. 215.

2. Ibid., p. 105.

3. Quoted in Kenneth Schneider, *Autokind vs. Mankind* (New York: Norton, 1971), p. 48.

2

State or Federal Financing

The immense importance of the automobile and truck in the modern American economy, coupled with the necessity of road construction, inevitably produced a powerful new force in national politics ... the "Highway Lobby." By the mid-twenties this new special interest group already exerted considerable power in the state houses and Congress, and its influence grew strong with the years. The Highway Lobby has long been comprised of a loose association of road contractors, state and federal highway officials, automobile clubs, trucking associations, automobile manufacturers, producers and suppliers of construction equipment and materials, engineers, oil companies, investment bankers and financial organizations, as well as many political figures with deep commitments to highway construction interests. One of the key organizations of the Highway Lobby is the American Road Builders Association, which has more than five thousand corporate and individual members representing all segments of the road construction industry. Over the years this organization effectively advocated the primacy of highway construction as opposed to federal subsidies to the railroads or urban transit systems. At the same time the Highway Lobby has provided interested local groups with "battle plans" to fight antifreeway groups; after 1956 it effectively protected the sanctity of the all-important Highway Trust Fund. Journalist Marquis Childs, a long-time observer of the Washington political scene, once aptly described the Highway Lobby as "the most powerful economic-political bloc in the nation ... a force that can move mountains, literally or figuratively."[1]

Eisenhower's Grand Plan

Several powerful forces thus converged during the early years of the Eisenhower administration. The time was ripe to launch the Interstate system that had been authorized in 1944, which Commissioner MacDonald of the Bureau of Public Roads had long been advocating. The urban street system and the major truck highways between cities were overwhelmed with traffic. The number of annual traffic fatalities each year produced cries of outrage from political leaders. And now that the Korean War had ended, and with it deep concern about inflation, the time for congressional action seemingly had arrived.

The question as it was perceived by congressional and administration leaders was not *whether* to build a new highway system, but *how*. The *how*

16

revolved around the method of financing. There was no doubt in the minds of national leaders, within either Congress or the Eisenhower administration, about the need for improved highways. No effort was made to distinguish between the need for improved travel *between* cities, and *within* them. Available documents indicate that the responsible people who should have known better allowed the two problems to be blurred into one (see Document 2). In the public dialogue no one sought to separate the question of improving intraurban travel (*Alternative 2*: see Document 4). Thus, what should have been a major topic of discussion—the role of urban mass transit—never received proper discussion or study at a crucial time. Highway Lobby spokesmen effectively prevented successful efforts to turn public attention to nonhighway concerns (see Documents 3, 4, and 5).

During the early fifties, a concerted lobbying effort by forty major organizations representing petroleum, rubber, trucking, automobile, and allied interest groups, called "Project Adequate Roads," conducted a vigorous publicity campaign through the media to educate the American people of the need for better highways. Dwight Eisenhower got the message loud and clear, and during the first eighteen months of his administration various committees wrestled with the problem. How to reconcile the divergent pressures? How to blend the conflicting views of farm groups, truckers, automobile manufacturers and state and federal highway engineers? How to satisfy state governors who adamantly opposed any method of financing that would force them to increase state taxes, while they simultaneously guarded their prior "right" to the tax upon gasoline? Several administration leaders, including Undersecretary for Transportation Robert Murray, and the Council of Economic Advisors' Public Works Director John S. Bragdon, strongly advocated a national toll road system; let those who use the highways pay for them, they argued. If the traffic was not heavy enough to generate sufficient tolls, then obviously a highway system was not needed. Conversely, the newly appointed commissioner of the Bureau of Public Roads, Frances V. du Pont, advocated one hundred percent federal financing, a sharp deviation from the traditional fifty-fifty formula that had existed since the days of Woodrow Wilson. Nearly everyone wanted a better highway system, but no one wanted to pay the cost.

Unable to get agreement from concerned interest groups, or for that matter, even within his administration, but acutely aware of the political urgency for positive action, Eisenhower decided to exert strong leadership. On July 12, 1954, he dispatched Vice-President Richard M. Nixon to the annual Governor's Conference at the resort community of Bolton Landing, New York to present his program (*Alternative 1*: see Document 2). His grand plan staggered the audience with its scope, because he advocated a master plan to facilitate farm-to-market travel and rapid intercity and interregional travel, as well as to alleviate traffic congestion within the metropolitan areas. He spelled out to the governors

> a grand plan for a properly articulated system that solves the problems
> of speedy, safe transcontinental travel—intercity transportation—access

highways—and   farm-to-farm   movement—metropolitan   area   congestion—bottlenecks—and parking.[2]

The president, well known for his grim determination to balance federal budgets, suggested the staggering figure of $5 billion annually for ten years, *in addition to* regular federal aid appropriations that now amounted to about $700 million annually.

Highways and Urban Revitalization

Beside itself with unrestrained joy, the Highway Lobby moved swiftly to capitalize upon the president's initiative. It enthusiastically endorsed Eisenhower's creation of a special advisory committee to be chaired by General Lucius Clay, one of the Cold War heroes of the Berlin Blockade. Now chairman of the board of the Continental Can Corporation, Clay carefully selected his committee members from well-recognized friends of the Highway Lobby: David Beck, head of the Teamsters Union; William A. Roberts, president of Allis Chalmers; Stephen D. Bechtel, a leading construction contractor; and Sloan Cclt of the Bankers Trust Company of New York City. These men were no enemies of the highway and the automobile (see Document 2).

During its hearings in early October, the Clay committee effectively restricted testimony to prohighway groups, and succeeded in ignoring the plaintive requests for a "balanced" transportation system from a token spokesman for the outnumbered transit interests (see Document 3). Chairman Clay set the tone of the hearings in his opening remarks: "We accept as a starting premise the fact that the penalties of an obsolete road system are large, and that the price in inefficiency is paid not only in dollars but in lives lost through lack of safety and also in national insecurity."[3] Yet the Clay committee had ample opportunity to consider a broader national transportation system within the scope of its inquiry. The role of urban transit kept surfacing during the hearings, even if in fact it did so inadvertently and contrary to Clay's wishes. In retrospect, it is difficult to comprehend why the committee did not pursue the question because of the vast amount of statistics that showed an overwhelmed urban street system. A long-time friend of urban expressways, Robert Moses, the famous and controversial New York City planner, told the committee that, "The needs of cities must not be minimized because they require relatively little mileage. This is strategic mileage of vital importance to both interstate and urban systems."[4]

Moses had long been an ardent exponent of the view that freeways must go *directly through* the urban areas and not merely connect cities. He carefully explained to the Clay committee that the great preponderance of automobile and truck trips both originated and terminated within the same metropolitan area. Because he strongly believed that the program was essential to the future of the American city in relationship to other programs aimed at economic and social revitalization, such as slum clearance, public housing, and urban redevelopment, he urged that the new highway program include ample financing for urban expressways. This vital urban link in the proposed interstate system, he said, required special attention:

> It is the hardest to locate, the most difficult to clear, the most expensive to acquire and build, and the most controversial from the point of view of selfish and short-sighted opposition. Without attempting to over-ride local opinion and dictate from distant capitals, the federal and state governments can help immeasurably to overcome local pressures by establishing engineering and other standards which can only be departed from at the risk of loss of federal and state aid of all kinds.[5]

No petty tyrant, this spokesman for the urban expressway builders; his message to the cities would be put simply and ruthlessly: either lace your cities with freeways or suffer the consequences of loss of *all* federal funding. Small wonder that in 1953 General Motors Corporation presented him with a $25,000 prize for the best essay on the need for adequate highways!

Moses, who had become a dominant figure in city planning circles (and who advocated freeways as the solution to urban problems), espoused the belief of planners that freeways held a key to revitalization of blighted areas. This belief had originated with one of the great pioneers of comprehensive urban planning, Harland Bartholomew, whose experience included consulting work for scores of major cities. As early as the 1920s, Bartholomew had become appalled by the unplanned and haphazard growth of cities, and he viewed carefully planned street and parkway construction as a useful means of controlling this destructive process. His philosophy that such development would insure "a sound, stable and orderly city structure" was echoed by the influential publisher of *American City*, Harold S. Buttenheim. The key to successful urban development, Buttenheim believed, was the incorporation of streets into a master plan that included zoning, redevelopment, public transit, slum clearance, and low-cost housing construction plans. Such an integrated plan, Bartholomew told the annual meeting of the American Institute of Planning, ultimately entailed a "balanced" urban transportation system. "City streets and highway systems cannot take the load, except in small cities. The price we are paying is too great for the results obtained. It is in the public interest from the standpoint of public convenience, public safety, and general economy of the community to concentrate on developing thoroughly sound mass transportation." This approach, he assured his audience,

> does not mean halting individual automobile traffic. It does mean restricting it where necessary for better accommodations for the majority of the traveling public. It does mean giving mass transportation first consideration as the basic and predominant means of transportation. It does mean restricting the automobile to its rightful place as a supplemental vehicle to be accommodated only after major transportation needs have been provided for.[6]

But by the mid-fifties such arguments were out of touch with the mood of the nation. The glorious heyday of the automobile was at hand. Most persons of influence viewed planning merely as a device to accommodate the automobile to the urban environment, not to subordinate its owner in any way to the needs of the city.

Adopting the traditional view of the nexus between highway construction and city planning, Harry A. Williams, a lobbyist for the Automobile Manufacturers Association, told a congressional committee in 1954 that, "These freeway networks are the only available method—let me repeat, the *only* available method—for redeveloping those parts of our central cities which have become blighted in coming years. Such freeways, coupled with major arterial routes feeding them, create neighborhood cells within which the city planner can work with confidence in redeveloping neighborhoods that have become structurally or functionally obsolete."[7]

This approach to urban planning was identical with that long advocated by the Bureau of Public Roads and its head, Thomas H. MacDonald. Ever since the early 1930s he had taken the position that highways were the key to urban regeneration. By the onset of the Second World War he already had in hand a master plan of interstate expressways tied to urban renewal. His master "Interregional Plan" of 1939 had even included urban radial and circumferential expressways. The plan was to ring the central business district of each city with expressways that were in turn connected to a national interregional highway system.

The Clay Committee Report: Ignoring the Alternatives

The testimony given the Clay committee in 1954 by Moses and several other profreeway witnesses raised serious questions about the problem of urban automobile congestion. The inference that *could* readily have been drawn from their testimony was the pressing need to reduce substantially the use of the automobile within metropolitan areas; yet the witnesses and the commission members blandly overlooked the possibility. The only concern of those providing testimony and committee members was to find means of permitting more and more automobiles to roam the metropolis (*Alternative 1*: see Documents 2, 3, 4, and 5).

Thus the Clay committee refused to recognize that it had two essentially different questions—that of intracity travel and that of intercity travel. That a national system of highways connecting major cities was necessary was beyond question; the only problem was one of working out the means of financing that would prove acceptable to several vitally interested pressure groups. Yet the committee also uncritically accepted the idea that the automobile was the *only* means of intracity travel. It did not probe the possibilities of commuter travel by means other than the automobile (*Alternative 2*: see Document 4). Especially, it did not pause to consider what urban freeways might do to existing subway, train, and bus systems, and nowhere did it consider the impact of the proposed highways upon the development of future systems. It did not consider what impact the construction of expressways would have upon the urban environment. Although recognizing that history provides twenty-twenty hindsight, and that such questions as these were not common in 1955, one may nonetheless contend that the committee's concept of its function was severely constricted and shortsighted.

The Clay Committee Report, submitted to the president early in January of 1955, concluded that the metropolitan areas needed expressways as soon as possible:

> Our cities have spread into suburbs, dependent on the automobile for their existence. The automobile has restored a way of life in which the individual may live in a friendly neighborhood, it has brought city and country closer together, it has made us one country and a united people. But America continues to grow. Our highway plan must similarly grow if we are to maintain and increase our standard of living. There can be no serious question as to the need for a more adequate highway system. Only the cost and how it is to be met poses a problem.[8]

No mention of other transportation alternatives was made. In fact, to highway officials, the alternative of public transit was irrelevant. As Federal Highways Administrator Francis Turner observed, "People have chosen to live in suburbia and exurbia, and whether this is good or bad is not a matter for highway and traffic engineers to decide. However, we do have an obligation to fashion a transportation system that will accommodate the choice which the people have made."[9]

Such assumptions as these clearly point up the fundamental weaknesses inherent in the thinking of the Eisenhower administration as well as Congress. The only problems recognized were the ones of financing. No concerns about the impact of the proposed highways upon urban life were manifest; the suburbanization of American cities was hailed as a sign of progress, and policy makers viewed their role as one of encouraging and facilitating the automobile's function in producing further urban sprawl (see Documents 2, 3, 4, and 5).

Although most of the city planners tended to view urban freeways as a means of revitalizing the central business district, the more practical dollar-conscious highway builders and suburban developers knew otherwise. To be sure, while some Eisenhower officials intended that the system should not intrude upon downtown areas, most administration insiders and highway lobbyists knew that they could make certain it did. For example, in the December, 1956 issue of *Automotive Industries*, it was enthusiastically pointed out that the new program would increase "pressure toward more and more decentralization. . . . The downtown commercial and industrial sites will become things of the past. In their place neighborhood units will spring up—pleasant residential areas, made up mostly of medium-size apartment buildings, located close to modern factories and office buildings, thus eliminating the need for a great deal of commuting." And apparently with this vision of Frank Lloyd Wright's Broadacre City in mind, the magazine told its readers, "In such an environment, the automobile would vastly increase its mobility and therefore become a more valuable part of urban living."[10]

The Highway Aid Act of 1956

Six weeks after receiving the Clay report, President Eisenhower sent to Congress in February of 1955 his special message on a national highway program (see Document 2). It essentially followed the Clay report, including the use of revenue bonds as the means of financing the federal portion of the cost; it also avoided the possibility of user toll charges, a policy General Clay said would produce "revolution" in the western states. The only influential voice with the administration on behalf of toll charges was General John S. Bragdon, a long-time friend of the president who now served as his Public Works administrator. General Bragdon firmly believed that the need for a new highway could readily be determined by the important test of whether its users would generate sufficient revenues to retire bonds by toll charges. Bragdon had admired the several toll highway programs already underway in many eastern and midwestern states, and he strongly advocated the incorporation of this concept in the new Interstate system. When the administration accepted Clay's opposition to tolls, Bragdon expressed his frustration in a memorandum to the Council of Economic Advisors: "So this ends the matter as far as toll roads are concerned. In other words, the American people will have a $37 billion bill for something which they could have gotten for nothing, all because of (a) political feasibility and (b), the horse and buggy anti-toll road sentiment in the Bureau of Public Roads."[11] Throughout the rest of the year, Congress wrangled over the means of financing the system, and ultimately it failed to pass legislation because several senators believed a proposed bonding concept was an illegal attempt to avoid the national debt ceiling. Democratic proposals to increase taxes upon trucking interests also produced predictable opposition from that influential industry.

In 1956, however, the pressures of traffic swell and the upcoming presidential election campaign forced the divergent interests to achieve a compromise solution. The chief architects of the compromises were two Democratic congressmen, George Fallon of Maryland, long recognized as one of the Highway Lobby's major supporters, and Hale Boggs of Louisiana (see Document 6). The pressure for the legislation was so great that the Congress passed the bill with only a single vote registered in opposition; in fact, the House passed the final bill by voice vote without debate. The lack of opposition led the *Saturday Evening Post*, itself no enemy of highways, to comment laconically upon the powers of the Highway Lobby, "That should answer any questions as who runs this country."[12]

The legislation created the National Systems Interstate and Defense Highway to be financed ninety percent by federal revenues and ten percent (sometimes reduced to five percent) by the states. The forty-one thousand mile system incorporated routes that connected nearly all American cities of fifty thousand or more. The highways were to be used not only for intercity travel, but also as the basic means of rapid travel within metropolitan areas. Construction was to be completed by 1972.

The major innovation of the 1956 Highway Act was the creation of the Highway Trust Fund. The fund would be created by federal taxes on lubricating oils and gasoline as well as excise taxes on buses and trucks. Thus the funds generated by the highway users themselves would be used to pay the cost of the new highway system. In addition, regular federal funds would continue to flow to the states and municipalities as part of existing construction programs. The Trust Fund was designed to satisfy the complaints of highway users that they were often taxed for nonhighway purposes. As Congressman Boggs commented, "For a great many years now highway users have complained, and I think with some justification . . . that vast revenues were being collected from them but were not being used for purposes of building highways. This bill recognized that complaint and it establishes the highway trust fund which dedicates most of those funds to highway construction and for that purpose only."[13] The Highway Lobby thus had succeeded in establishing a self-perpetuating construction financing system; each year the fund would expend several billions of dollars, and as road mileage increased, so too would automobile usage, thereby generating ever more revenue for the Trust Fund. Significantly, the law specified that the fund could not be used for purposes other than *new*. highway construction.

During the late sixties, when angry citizens' protests began to challenge the basic assumptions of urban freeway policy, it was the Trust Fund that became the focal point of controversy (see Document 9). Because of its self-perpetuating nature, the critics saw it as the result of a conspiracy of the Highway Lobby to continue building freeways whether or not they were either wanted or needed. It would continue to pump billions each year into highway construction *independent* of the Congress, and thereby deprive such social enterprises as education and public welfare of crucial funds; it would also deprive transit systems of adequate funds. As one of the most outspoken critics, A. Q. Mowbray, explained, the Trust Fund was "a perfect closed loop calculated to keep smiles on the faces of the highway builders." Since the fund was virtually removed from congressional supervision, "each year the Administration holds out the bounty to the states as their highway departments come up with plans that seem reasonable to the Federal Bureau of Public Roads. As the road mileage increases, more cars take to the roads and drive more miles, burning more gallons of gasoline, wearing out more tires, and feeding more money into the inviolate Trust Fund." Thus, during the 1960s, Mowbray concludes, "The money poured into the Highway Trust Fund in a golden stream. Engineers across the land drew lines on maps, and the bulldozers followed, in increasing numbers. While each year Washington budgetmakers strained to find the money for a thousand crying needs, and Congressional committee rooms echoed to the voices pleading for funds to pour on this or that hurt, the inviolable Highway Trust Fund plowed ahead under its own power, the money pouring in one end and out the other, as though regulated by an immutable law of nature."[14]

No less angry about the impact of freeways upon the quality of life in urban America was Helen Leavitt, an angry housewife whose best-selling panegryic *Superhighway-Superhoax* (1970) stirred public comment and infuriated highway lobbyists. "Highway officials argue that they are for a 'balanced transportation system,' which means that they will support mass transit systems as long as they can build all the highways they wish. If the congressional guardians of the Highway Trust Fund truly believe in providing transportation, they will be willing to allow trust fund money to finance whichever mode of transportation a community chooses." The opposite, of course, was the case. "Instead, they showed that highway taxes are collected to build highways only and that the motoring public is paying for them, not subway systems or any other form of transportation." Ms. Leavitt, zeroing in on the fact that the Trust Fund could not be used for anything except new highway construction, sputtered angrily, "If it is justifiable to use gasoline taxes exclusively for highway construction, the federal tax on alcohol should be spent to promote and expand the liquor industry" (see Document 9).

The Impact on Urban Life

The impassioned attack upon the Trust Fund, however, came only after the urban freeways had altered the nature of life in America's cities. Few Americans in 1956 had the insight and sensitivity for the nature and function of urban life as did Lewis Mumford. A few months after the passage of the National Highway Aid Act in 1956, Mumford sadly concluded that, "The most charitable thing to assume about this [(legislation)] is that they hadn't the faintest notion of what they were doing." With unerring prophetic insight, Mumford wrote that, "Within the next fifteen years they will doubtless find out; but by that time it will be too late to correct all the damage to our cities and our countryside, to say nothing of all the efficient organization of industry and transportation, that this ill-conceived and absurdly unbalanced program will have wrought."[15] A few years later, Wilfred Owen in commenting upon the growing dependence of the American metropolis upon the automobile, asked "whether it is possible to be urbanized and motorized and at the same time civilized?"[16]

Although few were willing to confront the penetrating criticism of Mumford and the crucial question raised by Owen, events during the 1960s would lead ultimately to significant public disaffection from both the urban freeway and the automobile.

By the early seventies, as James Flink points out in a perceptive analysis of the impact of "automobility" upon the American consciousness, the motor car had lost its solid base of popular support: "By the 1960s, the transformation of American civilization by the motorcar was virtually completed, and motoring had lost much of its earlier romance. . . . A new generation of Americans, reared in an automobile culture, could accept the automobile revolution as a mundane part of the establishment and turn to more pressing problems: world peace, poverty, civil rights and ecology." Ironically, Flink points out, "Much of this new generation's energy promises to be channeled into coping with unanticipated consequences of the automobile revolution: environmental pollution, urban sprawl, the decay of the center city, the decimation of our remaining wilderness area and free-flowing streams, and the malfunctionings of oligopoly" (see Document 6)[17]

Certainly part of the disaffection with the automobile stemmed from the popular "antiestablishment" culture; the high-powered, large sedans symbolized to youthful rebels the extravagance and misplaced priorities of American civilization. To some the automobile industry and its slick mystique of annual model changes and high-pressure sales promotions reflected the mistaken and irrelevant values of a bourgeois society. To them, the lack of concern demonstrated by automobile manufacturers for passenger safety, as charged by consumer advocate and crusader against unethical corporate practices Ralph Nader, raised serious questions regarding the public role of the industry.

This type of criticism in the late sixties contributed to a rapidly growing spirited attack upon urban freeways. Public reaction, however, did not follow ideological or political lines, but instead resulted from the failure of the freeways to live up to public expectations or to the grandiose claims made on their behalf by the Highway Lobby. Further, the freeways produced several unexpected and undesirable side effects which intensified criticism. Opposition usually took the form of citizens' committees seeking to halt new freeway construction, but it led ultimately to a concerted assault upon the Highway Lobby's most sacred vestal—the Trust Fund (see Document 12). Unlike many protest movements in American history, this movement defied generalizations about the racial, regional, ethnic, political, sexual, or class composition of its protesters. They came from all such possible groups. Freeway opponents crossed all demographic lines to produce temporary political alliances, usually in the form of *ad hoc* citizens' committees, to achieve specific objectives—normally the halting of construction.

Behind the protests, however, there existed a growing dissatisfaction with the automobile as the major means of urban transportation (see Documents 6 and 8). As it made increasing demands for ever more urban land for new freeways, huge cloverleaf interchanges, wider streets and, especially, additional parking spaces, the conception began to grow in the minds of some critical observers that the city was no longer designed for man, but was being rebuilt to accommodate the needs of the automobile. Typical of this growing dissatisfaction with the automobile in the city were the observations by the internationally prominent urban planner and transportation expert, Wilfred Owen:

> Where all-out efforts have been made to accommodate the car, the streets are still congested, commuting is increasingly difficult, urban aesthetics have suffered, and the quality of life has been eroded. In an automotive age, cities have become the negation of communities—a setting for machines instead of people. The automobile has taken over, motorist and non-motorist alike are caught up in the congestion, and everyone is a victim of the damaging effects of the conflict between the

car and the community. The automobile is an irresistible force that may become an immovable object, and in the process destroy the city.[18]

During its final year in office, the Eisenhower administration also became deeply concerned. Costs were skyrocketing, and expressway design presented thorny problems. But the construction of the Interstate system within the cities proved to be the crucial problem. Public Works Administrator Bragdon, who had consistently and adamantly opposed the intrusion of the system in the heart of the cities, pointed out early in 1960 that, "Taking care of local needs in cities should not include providing for rush-hour traffic nor solving local traffic bottleneck problems. To do so will generally defeat the basic aim of the Interstate System. . . . The urgent traffic needs in urban areas should not be met through alteration of the primary objectives of the Interstate System." Yet, the cities had recognized a golden opportunity to solve their transit needs by tapping the Highway Trust Fund; and despite the president's opposition to what he viewed as a distortion of the intent of the Interstate concept, the cities prevailed. This was well summarized in a memorandum after a meeting of highway officials by an assistant to Bragdon in late 1960:

> There are increasing tendencies to use the Interstate System as the main solution to suburban commuter transportation problems in metropolitan areas without adequate consideration of suitable or possibly better alternatives. Differences of opinion emerged as to whether parts of this program were being directed more at attempts to solve purely local problems than at advancing basic national objectives. There is concern that some of the new freeways being provided by the Interstate Program might be strangled in their own traffic on opening day. . . . Lack of adequate progress in overall planning, particularly land use and mass transportation planning in urban areas, was evident.[19]

The freeways, of course, were merely the most recent effort to accommodate the city to the automobile. . . . and in an ever widening circle the American people were not satisfied with either. Yet by the 1970s the failures of earlier generations left a disaffected population without acceptable immediate alternatives (see Document 7). By destroying the nineteenth-century walking city and by setting in motion a pattern of decentralization and sprawl, the typical urban resident could not survive without daily access to an automobile. It had become an absolute necessity.

Notes

1. Quoted in Charlton Ogburn, "The Motorcar vs. America," *American Heritage*, June, 1970, p. 105.

2. *New York Times*, July 13, 1954, p. 1.

3. Clay Commission Papers, Dwight D. Eisenhower Library, Abilene, Kansas.

4. Ibid.

5. Ibid.

6. "Planning for Metro Transport," *Planning and Civic Comment*, September, 1954, p. 4.

7. Quoted in A. Q. Mowbray, *Road to Ruin* (Philadelphia: Lippincott, 1969), p. 95.

8. Clay Commission Papers, Eisenhower Library.

9. Quoted in Kenneth Schneider, *Autokind vs. Mankind* (New York: Norton, 1971), p. 68.

10. Quoted in Helen Leavitt, *Superhighway—Superhoax* (New York: Doubleday, 1970), p. 3.

11. Bragdon to Council of Economic Advisors, Feb. 1, 1955, John S. Bragdon Papers, Eisenhower Library.

12. Robert Thruelson, "Coast to Coast Without Stopping," *Saturday Evening Post*, October 20, 1956, p. 23.

13. Quoted in Mark Howard Rose, "Express Highway Politics, 1939-1956" (Ph.D. dissertation, Ohio State University, 1973), p. 264.

14. Quoted in Mowbray, *Road to Ruin*, p. 21.

15. Lewis Mumford, *The Highway and the City* (New York: Harcourt, Brace and World, 1963), p. 234.

16. Wilfred Owen, *The Metropolitan Transportation Problem* (Washington, D.C.: Brookings Institution, 1956), p. 81.

17. James J. Flink, "Three Stages of American Automobile Consciousness," *American Quarterly*, October, 1972, p. 473.

18. Wilfred Owen, *The Accessible City* (Washington, D.C.: Brookings Institution, 1972), p. 1.

19. Floyd Papperson to Bragdon, September 28, 1960, Bragdon Papers, Eisenhower Library.

3

City or Suburb

The decline in urban mass transit systems began during the 1920s as a consequence of the enthusiastic acceptance by the American people of the automobile. Thanks to improved technology, it had become a reliable form of transportation that most working Americans could afford. Passenger mileage on commuter trains and subways began to level off during the 1920s, and during the fifteen-year span covering depression and war these systems were allowed to deteriorate. By 1948, when automobile manufacturers had resumed domestic production, the more recently established bus lines also encountered problems. A vicious cycle set in; with revenues declining, transit authorities had to cut back on their service; schedules were pared and equipment deteriorated because much needed replacements could not be purchased. Travel on commuter trains fell from thirty-two billion passenger miles in 1950 to less than eight billion in 1970. Buses themselves became ensnarled in rush hour traffic, and the advantages of commuting by public transit were further reduced. The resulting poor service, in turn, forced additional commuters to the use of the private automobiles. The new expressways further encouraged the use of the automobile for urban travel and in essence provided a *coup de grace* to urban transit systems. By the 1960s, in only a very few metropolitan areas did a majority of central city workers arrive by public transit. Nationwide studies revealed that three-fourths or more of all urban workers traveled daily to work by private automobile.

The intolerable level of rush hour traffic forced city planners to take action. And in every city in the nation (partially excepting San Francisco) the solution was to find a means of increasing the daily flow of automobiles. Thus America's urban leaders embraced the 1956 Highway Aid Act with enthusiasm, not only because it contained what seemed to be the appropriate solution, but also because it included the new magic formula of ninety percent federal funding. Upon its passage, highway engineers and city officials busied themselves planning for the Great Solution. By the early 1960s stretches of the expressways were opened to the public, and by 1974, seven thousand miles of urban freeways were in use throughout the nation.

The Shaping of Suburban Life

Without exception, the impact was the same. The expressways greatly accelerated the movement to the suburbs. Urban sprawl now became a definite pattern radiating out from the new expressways; real estate developers found "easy access" to the nearby interchange an attractive feature to new subdivision home buyers. Then came the new shopping centers to provide convenient shopping, and in their wake, new office buildings. Not only did the suburban environment provide an opportunity for attractive landscaping of business buildings, but employees could also drive to work and entirely avoid the congestion and unpleasantness of the central city. Manufacturers also found the low prices of land attractive, because they could now build single-level assembly plants which were much more efficient than the multistoried ones that high central city land prices had demanded. On the heels of the manufacturers came the warehouses and truck terminals at the convergence of two interstate highways, usually on the edge of a metropolis.

Not far away there also appeared, like so many mushrooms after a spring rain, the innumerable chain restaurants and motor hotels designed to reap the benefits resulting from a nation on wheels. While these new innovations of the great Asphalt Age flourished, business in the central city declined. Located in the heart of the city (near the once-busy railroad station), the stately hotels of earlier generations suffered heavy losses. Unless they were among the very few large enough to attract national conventions, they frequently had to close. Many were even razed to make way for "progress"— often in the form of a new parking lot. Downtown merchants also suffered, undercut by the sparkling new shopping centers.

The automobile was thus both cause and effect of the massive growth of the American suburbs following the Second World War. The automobile provided the means of dispersal; suburban growth prior to the automobile had radiated out along the tracks of the horse car or trolley lines. Yet the use of the automobile by commuters so clogged the city streets that it drove both employer and employee to the less congested suburbs. In 1970 the Bureau of the Census noted the fact that the steady outward movement had resulted in more Americans living in the suburban areas of the metropolitan areas than in the central cities. Few major cities in 1970 could boast of significant population increases since 1930, so heavy had been the exodus to "Happy Knolls" or "Greenwood Estates." "Virtually all the metropolitan growth between 1960 and 1970 occurred outside the central cities, where a majority of the metropolitan residents now live," the Census bureau reported.[1]

To be certain, as many scholars and journalists have noted, the suburban migration grew out of many factors: dislike for the congestion and confusion of the central city; a fear of violence; the attractions (which often proved temporary) of lower land prices and much lower property taxes; a longing for more living space and clean air; and a desire to escape the growing number of poor blacks who were moving into the central cities in large numbers (see Document 9).

The suburbs were designed for the automobile. Churches, schools, and stores were almost always beyond walking distances. So were places of employment. In fact, the active suburban family with children found *two* cars a virtual necessity for its daily pattern of existence, thereby increasing traffic problems. Another lamentable side effect of the industrial and business development in the suburbs was that it also placed new burdens upon unskilled central city workers, who frequently found themselves forced into the use of the automobile for "reverse commuting"—that is, driving to a distant suburb to work and returning in the evening to their house or apartment. The illogic of it all staggers the imagination.

Disintegration of the Cities

Traffic planners also discovered, much to their chagrin, that the freeways did not necessarily reduce traffic congestion. As critic John Jerome points out: "Freeways make congestion.... Freeways attract cars like magnets, pulling traffic off the secondary roads and local streets. Freeways funnel local traffic, in search of convenience, into the streams of long-haul through traffic for which the freeways were originally planned."[2] Despite the fact that one can travel rapidly during off-peak hours, bottlenecks develop during morning and evening rush hours because "traffic is, in the end, simply dumped, at whatever destination inspired the building of the highway in the first place. Six lanes into two, the bottleneck sending waves of congestion rippling back out the freeway to close off the very freeness for which it was created." As Jerome observes, "nothing works. The most elaborate and carefully wrought plans, when converted into concrete, suddenly bulge with overloads in wrong places, sucking cars seemingly out of thin air and giving them nowhere to go. Attempting to reduce congestion simply by spreading cars out over more roadway is like attempting to avoid drowning by brushing back the sea."[3]

By reshaping the urban environment on a basis of population dispersal, the engineers' efforts tended to increase automobile usage. Thus the freeways quickly carried a traffic load far in excess of that which was anticipated; for example, engineers had designed the Los Angeles Harbor Freeway to carry a maximum of 100,000 cars a day when it opened in 1954; by 1956 it already averaged 168,000 a day. In many cities rush hour freeway traffic slowed to a crawl, while cars on the side streets likewise backed up into a hopeless snarl.

As the freeways dumped more and more cars into the central business district during the working days, the pressures upon existing parking space increased. Consequently, high-rise parking garages became a familiar part of the downtown scene; older buildings were razed to accommodate the need for more parking space. By the late 1960s most American cities had devoted one-third or more of their downtown space for automobile parking. Not only did parking take up vast acreage, but an additional twenty percent of the downtown was consumed by streets, alleys, freeways, and enormous "cloverleaf" interchanges. "A parking map or aerial photo of any American city center reveals devastation as obvious as that resulting from the London Blitz," urban expert Kenneth Schneider wrote in 1971. "Saturation bombing is the only adequate comparison. Hundreds of buildings around the immediate center had been wiped out. In that photo the rubble seemed to have been cleared by vast bands of beetles [automobiles] who wait disciplined and ready in the empty blocks to clear the debris of unbombed sections. Others are already on the move in the streets."[4]

Urban freeways also worked to reduce the amount of low-cost housing available to the urban poor. Simply put, the poor tend to concentrate near the city's core because this is where the largest amount of low-cost housing is available. It has traditionally been in these areas that shortsighted and ill-conceived federally funded slum clearance and urban renewal projects have been used to "clear" dilapidated buildings. Often, as many studies have demonstrated, these projects uprooted viable neighborhoods and reduced even further the amount of less expensive housing available in a city. While city agencies enthusiastically ripped down these "blighted" housing areas near the city core in an attempt to revitalize the overall economy of the area, they failed to build sufficient public housing in their place. As historian Sam Bass Warner, Jr., observes,

> By an unhappy convergence of history, the interstate highway program passed Congress in an era of political reaction, so that the seizure of poor urban neighborhoods coincided with a cutback in public housing. Since the location of roads just outside the urban center was implicit in the wheel strategy of the highway engineer, the cry of 'blight' urged on him the merits of taking as much of the land as he wished. Thus to rip out the houses of the poor was a transportation principle that became a public contribution rather than an act of social irresponsibility.[5]

Thus, it has been demonstrated many times that the enormous land needs of the highways near the city center worked to the direct disadvantage of the housing needs of the city's poor.

As public criticism of these many counterproductive effects began to mount, spokesmen for the automobile and highway interests responded that because the American people were still buying more cars each year and demanding better highways, this in itself justified the existing urban highway system. In essence, they argued a *fait accompli* had decided matters. Because the American people were *already* dependent upon the automobile, government should thereby continue with its ongoing construction program (*Alternative 1*: see Documents 6 and 8). In an important address in 1966 in New Orleans, Henry Ford II argued, "When so many people buy our products, the automobile industry must be doing something right." In response to calls for massive new programs in urban transit systems, he said, "Some of our critics seem to feel that the government should plan cities and transportation to reflect their own conception of the ideal city, regardless of what people prefer. This is nonsense. . . . As far as urban transportation is concerned, what people want is clear. They have voted overwhelmingly in favor of the automobile." To this important spokesman for the automobile and highway forces, the people's "vote" was sufficient; the objective of city planning should therefore be "to develop better ways of giving people what they want and are willing to pay for" (see Document 6). However, within a few more years, Mr. Ford and his associates would discover that an increasing number of Americans would be willing to pay for urban transit; they especially did not wish to pay for additional urban freeways.

The Growth of Public Disenchantment

During the early years of the construction of the Interstate system, little public criticism developed because most of the construction occurred in the rural areas and affected few persons directly. To be certain, conservation and environmental spokesmen raised impassioned pleas against the destruction of forests or mountains, but few persons responded. However, when construction began in earnest in urban areas, protest erupted. It often came from unlikely sources. Because the highway planners and engineers followed long-established construction principles and proposed to build the new expressways through unpopulated areas within the metropolitan regions, their plans frequently called for the penetration of what little natural terrain remained in the cities . . . along riverbeds, across parks, over tree-covered hills and through rugged ravines. Naturalists and environmentalists were appalled, and quickly mobilized their forces to stop the proposed constructions.

It was inevitable, however, that many residential areas would be invaded by the highways. Quite naturally, those residential areas close to the central business district were most vulnerable as the several expressways converged at the city's center; in most instances, these areas were inhabited by the poor, quite often of minority stock. In city after city, highway planners instinctively selected the lower income neighborhoods for the paths of their new routes, perhaps realizing that these residents had less political influence and were less likely to organize an effective protest. Residents of condemned areas, it became apparent, did not agree with a 1956 comment in *Saturday Evening Post* about the great benefits of the recently created Interstate system: "The dissident minorities who find themselves in the path of this interchange or that expressway can help if they would stop to realize that every foot of the new highway is necessary for the national well-being."[6] In Nashville, as one classic example, "national well-being" required that I-40 slice through the black neighborhood on the northwest side of the city, leaving more than fifty dead end streets, forever dividing what had been a cohesive neighborhood. In other cities, the new freeways threatened historical landmarks, including the French Quarter in New Orleans, Fishermens' Wharf in San Francisco, and lovely Overton Park and Zoo in Memphis. Thus a common foe helped forge an unusual political alliance among members of racial minorities in defense of their homes, representatives of the upper class seeking to preserve historic landmarks or public parks, and middle-class whites who feared possible decline in the property values of their homes.

Throughout the nation, impassioned citizens' protests forced major revision or even abandonment of construction plans. By the early 1970s it was estimated that some four hundred different controversies had occurred in American cities as a result of opposition or proposed or actual freeway construction.

The first such opposition protests occurred, quite ironically (or perhaps as a consequence), in the American city with the highest concentration of automobiles in the nation (seven thousand per square mile). San Francisco residents not only showed other cities the way to fight the freeways, but also pioneered in the creation—in a semirelated development—of a modernistic mass transit system (BART) (*Alternative 2:* see Document 11). The eight-lane, double-decked, elevated Embarcadero Freeway (sixty-two feet above the ground) is today probably the most famous stretch of freeway in the world, and it does not carry a single vehicle. The biggest problem it currently presents to city leaders is how to raise the estimated $15 million to tear it down. When construction began in 1959, government officials skipped the usual ceremonial fanfare, because angry protests had already surfaced. Opposition grew primarily from the fact that the freeway would shut off for many residents the view of their beloved bay. Thus the half-constructed Embarcadero still stands today, looming over the bay like a huge concrete ski jump, mute testimony to the power mobilized by antifreeway sentiment in "The City."

Since that time, attempts to complete the Embarcadero as an underground highway have been defeated, and two other proposed freeways were voted down by the county Board of Supervisors by a vote of six to five in the wake of strong protest movements. In 1969 San Francisco mayor Joseph Allioto told a public gathering that no more freeways would be built: "San Francisco, truly one of the majestic cities in the world, is not going to be turned into a wasteland of freeways and garages."

"People Before Highways"

Meanwhile, on the other coast, freeway construction had created similar convulsive political turmoil. Proposals during the sixties to extend the Interstate system into the heart of Boston had been met with concerted opposition; Harvard professors locked arms with factory workers to combat the plans of the Bureau of Public Works to run the highway through Cambridge. Mayor Kevin White joined forces with the group and at a crucial time in early 1969, a massive "People Before Highways" protest demonstration before the State House in Boston attracted national attention. That same year highway enthusiast and former Massachusetts Governor John Volpe had just assumed his new position as Secretary of the Department of Transportation within the Nixon administration, and he promised highway backers that the much-delayed Boston Inner Belt through Cambridge would soon be under construction. However, growing opposition within the city—and the powerful logic of their arguments—impressed the new governor, Francis Sargent, who had previously served as associate director of the Massachusetts Department of Public Works under Governor Volpe; his enthusiasm for freeways had earned him the reputation as "the road builder." During the early period of the planning, he told a press conference, "This road is the key to the entire Massachusetts transportation system. It has to be built, with as little disruption as possible, and it has to be designed as attractively as possible. We'll be working hard to get the necessary approval for this road." Deeply aware of growing popular opposition, in 1965 he attempted, unsuccessfully, to have the legislature remove veto powers by local communities over interstate highway construction within their borders.

Thus, when Sargent replaced Volpe in the Governor's Mansion in 1969, antifreeway leaders saw little light at the end of the tunnel. Yet the new Republican governor responded sympathetically to the growing tide of local opposition. He also recognized the growing concern nationwide for the impact of expressways upon urban areas. The Greater Boston Committee on the Transportation Crisis convinced him that the Inner Belt should not be built. In February of 1970, the governor repudiated his former public reputation as an ardent highway booster, and announced that he had requested Secretary Volpe to remove the project from the list of federal requests. The costs in terms ·of demolished homes, shattered neighborhoods, and environmental damages, he said, were too great. The state of Massachusetts, he had concluded, simply could better spend its transportation funds in other ways. And, in a rare admission for a public figure, he told the people of the state on a television broadcast, "Nearly everyone was sure highways were the only answer to transportation problems for years to come. But we were wrong."[7]

Throughout the United States, disenchantment with urban expressways was growing. The Massachusetts governor's admission, "But we were wrong," a rare instance of candor and courage for a major elected official, evoked sympathetic response elsewhere. In city after city, court cases or administrative decisions stopped highway construction. "Today it is almost impossible to get a major Interstate project approved in most cities," a leading economic reporter observed in *Fortune Magazine* in 1971. These cities included Chicago, Hartford, Providence, Philadelphia, New York, Baltimore, Washington, D.C., Memphis, Nashville, Shreveport, Cleveland, San Antonio and Seattle.[8] Even in Los Angeles freeway advocates had become pessimistic.

The rapidly growing metropolitan area of Phoenix came to the freeway business relatively late. The Black Canyon Freeway, built in the early sixties, slices around the western and southern edge of the city as part of the Interstate system program connecting Los Angeles to New Orleans; however, this highway does not serve the area of heaviest population growth on the eastern edge of the metropolis, and consequently state highway officials proposed construction of the Papago Freeway, which would cut through the heart of the metropolitan area on an east-west axis. Powerful economic interests provided enthusiastic support because the Papago would connect the affluent suburbs in Scottsdale, Mesa, and Tempe to the Phoenix central business district. By the time the project surfaced in 1972, however, Phoenicians had behind them several years of experience over environmental concerns. Heavy automobile-produced smog had threatened the city's lucrative winter tourist business, and several battles had been waged over real estate development of the beautiful mountains that surround the city. An opposition group, led by relatively wealthy citizens, launched a vigorous opposition crusade. Surprisingly it was tacitly joined by the powerful *Arizona Republic*. This staunchly conservative newspaper ran a series of essays about freeway problems in other cities, urged the alternatives of some form of mass transit, praised bicycle paths, and provided a forum in its columns for antifreeway spokesmen.

The Papago Inner Loop, which would have extended into downtown Phoenix, drew the heaviest fire because it included the amazing feature of more than a mile of highway elevated nearly one hundred feet above the city! This engineer's dream, however, struck many citizens as a nightmare. Views of the lovely desert mountains that surround the city would have been blocked for thousands, and the already existing north-south split between white middle-class Phoenicians and "south side" minorities would have been accentuated. The proposed elevated highway, more than any other factor of the project, led to a resounding defeat for the freeway advocates in an advisory referendum conducted by the city government. This victory for the antihighway forces led to the temporary abandonment of the entire Papago project, although in 1974 resilant highway proponents were once more preparing their plans. Whether or not they could make a comeback in the face of public opposition and an acute local gasoline shortage remained to be seen. At least for the present, Phoenix had joined in a national movement against overreliance upon the automobile as the means of urban travel.

The Plight of Mass Transit

The rising tide of opposition to the urban expressways and a marked disaffection with the large American automobile that accompanied the sudden shortage of gasoline in late 1973 gave impetus toward a reconsideration of the nation's transportation strategy. A begrudging national recognition that overreliance upon the automobile had been extremely wasteful of fuel when compared to that necessary to operate a fleet of buses or a commuter train system, bestirred long exasperated transit advocates with renewed hope.

Yet the sudden crisis-provoked enthusiasm for mass transit did not provide reasons for expecting success. The automobile-highway-oil juggernaut remained extraordinarily powerful, and the American love affair with the automobile remained very much in evidence. Transit enthusiasts knew that great hurdles lay before them during the 1970s, and that tremendous technical, economic, and social problems needed to be solved. For example, they knew that nearly two generations of Americans had been born since the better days of mass transit systems, they knew the inherent political power of the Highway Lobby, and they knew especially of the reluctance of the urban commuter to abandon his beloved private car. Studies had further shown that commuters were extremely reluctant to pay fares equal to operational costs of a system, even though those fares nonetheless remained well below the daily costs of operating a private automobile. A fare increase of five or ten cents, experience had shown, would be sufficient to drive the commuter back to his automobile. However, much larger increases in automobile insurance and gasoline would not have the reverse effect. Thus spokesmen for mass transit recognized that federal subsidies for the operation of transit systems in order to keep fares down was virtually essential (*Alternative 2*: see Document 10). Yet on this point they encountered fierce congressional and state house opposition; it was one thing to use federal funds to subsidize the automobile industry to the tune of some $20 billion a year in highway construction and maintenance, but something much different to subsidize public transit companies.

The plight of urban mass transit in the 1970s can be readily summarized: ever since the years immediately following the Second World War, all urban transit systems have lost passengers (see Document 10). This has resulted not only from the immense popularity of the automobile, but also from the overwhelming impact of federal policy that served the highway interest at the expense of both urban transit systems and railroads. Between 1947 and 1970, the federal government spent $58 billion on highways, $12 billion on airport construction and airline subsidies, and even an additional $6 billion for waterway development. In contrast to this enormous outlay of funds, it spent only the meagre sum of $795 million on urban mass transit. Is it any wonder that in the 1970s the nation found itself without adequate mass transit programs?

Totally absorbed with the express highway, the Eisenhower administration ignored the nation's declining transit systems. To be certain, President Eisenhower himself opposed the intrusion of the Interstate system into the central cities, but his highway officials readily overcame or sidestepped his opposition. During the Kennedy years, the first glimmering of concern for mass transit can be found in the Housing Act of 1961. One section of this omnibus legislation called for "comprehensive urban transportation surveys, studies, and plans to aid in solving problems of traffic congestion, facilitating the circulation of people and goods in metropolitan and other urban areas, and reducing transportation need." The $75 million authorized under this act to facilitate planning and demonstration grants contrasts vividly with the more than $5 billion being expended each year on the Interstate system from the Highway Trust Fund (and this does not include other federal highway programs and state and local street and highway expenditures). Yet it was, however limited, a beginning.

In 1964 President Lyndon Johnson urged upon the Congress the importance of urban transit programs: "In the next forty years we must completely renew our cities. The alternative is disaster. Gaping needs must be met in health, in education, in job opportunities, in housing. And not a single one of these needs can be fully met until we rebuild our mass transportation systems."[9] Congress responded feebly with the Urban Transportation Act of 1964, which authorized the expenditure of the modest figure of $375 million by 1968, "to provide additional assistance for the development of comprehensive and coordinated mass transportation systems, both public and private, in metropolitan and other urban areas." This program, however, was little more than a faint expression of good intentions. In 1966 Johnson discovered just how powerful the Highway Lobby was when he sought merely to delay the distribution of some $1 billion in Highway Trust monies as a means of curbing inflation. He was overwhelmed by the highwaymen in Congress, and with several of his favorite legislative measures threatened by congressional retaliation, he hurriedly released the funds. Johnson, none-theless, had determined that improved mass transit was vital for the future of the American metropolis and noted this decision in an important message to Congress on March 2, 1966 (*Alternative 2*: see Document 7).

Federal Aid for Mass Transit

As public opposition to the urban expressways mounted during the late sixties, pressures began to develop to tap the Trust Fund for mass transit programs (*Alternative 2*: see Document 12). Some advocated the creation of a new Mass Transit Trust Fund, but Congress remained unmoved. Yet cracks in the wall were beginning to appear. In 1970 Congress passed the Urban Mass Transportation Act which authorized $10 billion for nonhighway construc-tion by 1982; however, it failed to appropriate the funds. Thus in 1970 the United States government spent just $161 million on urban mass transit, $215 million in 1971, and $375 million in 1972. Meanwhile, the multibillion dollar highway construction program rolled resolutely—yet with less confidence—forward.

Quite likely historians in the future will look upon 1972 as the turning point in federal transportation policy. In March of that year Transportation Secretary John Volpe announced his plan to tap the Highway Trust Fund for mass transit purposes, while several other top Nixon administration officials made sounds about the importance of developing urban mass transit. "The problem is not how much we have spent on highways in the past, but how very little we have spent on public transportation," Volpe said.[10] The one-time highway enthusiast from Massachusetts had had a change of heart. In 1972 Congress cracked the Trust Fund by authorizing the expenditure of $800 million dollars for mass transit research. The Congress, at the same time, extended the life of the Trust Fund until 1977, but it was understood by all that it would expire at that time. Perhaps most significant of all, Democratic Congressman George Fallon of Maryland, the creator of the Trust Fund and its long-time guardian and protector, was defeated in his bid for reelection.

Then came the "energy crisis." As gasoline suddenly fell to short supply, and with some 112 million automobiles dependent upon it, public officials began to recognize the extreme wastefulness of precious fuel reserves by the overdependence upon the automobile. Suddenly, mass transit was "hot," and officials scrambled to get aboard the popular bandwagon. By early February of 1974, the Nixon administration had taken the initiative, and the president sent to Congress a major $19 billion program for urban transit by 1980 (*Alternative 2*: see Document 13). Nixon candidly admitted that although the program had been under consideration for some time, the sudden crunch at the gasoline pumps had given the program new urgency. "The energy crisis has underscored an important lesson: Our system of national transportation is not working at maximum efficiency." The proposal would constitute "the largest federal commitment ever to the improvement of public transportation in our cities and towns," the president said. By 1977 the total outlay of block grants to urban areas would approach the $3 billion figure, and at that time the controversial Highway Trust Fund would expire and an entirely new unified approach to funding of all transportation programs, both mass transit and highway construction would be established.

Thus, not only did Nixon's proposal include the elimination of the Trust Fund, but also sought the establishment of a central transportation funding program to deal with the many different, but related, transportation problems of the United States. Consistent with Nixon's pragmatic conservatism, the burden of decision making and implementation would be at the local level: "Two-thirds of this amount ($19 billion) would be allocated to state and local governments for application in areas where they believe this money can be spent most effectively," he said in a nationwide radio address. "This could entail construction of highways or public transit systems, or the purchase of buses or rail cars" (*Alternative 2 and 3*: see Document 13).

Nixon's proposal, which Congress seemed certain to adopt at least in some modified form in 1974, left mass transit leaders both elated and disappointed. While the clear intent was to encourage development of urban mass transit, Nixon nonetheless left the door wide open for the utilization of the funds for additional expressway construction, if that were the decision of local officials. Yet, from the perspective of the mid-seventies, the Nixon message amounted to a major turning point for the forces of a balanced urban transportation system. It certainly stood light years away from the dismal days of the 1950s.

An Experiment in Urban Mass Transit: BART

As the nation began to reexamine its assumptions about urban transit policy, the notable effort in the San Francisco Bay Area took on new meaning and significance (*Alternative 2*: see Document 11). The Bay Area Rapid Transit (BART) system had its origins in 1947 when a team of army and navy engineers recommended an underwater trans-bay tube to carry a commuter train and link Oakland and San Francisco as the best means of alleviating the growing traffic pressure in the bay region. In 1951 the state legislature established the San Francisco Bay Rapid Transit Commission, which had representatives from nine Bay Area counties. The commission agreed that a rapid transit system was crucial to the environmental future of the lovely Bay Area, and by 1956 had issued initial plans detailing a rail system encircling the bay from San Jose to the south to Santa Rosa and Napa to the north. The legislature then created a Bay Area Rapid Transit District, and in 1959 three engineering firms began to prepare detailed plans for the planned 123 mile system.

The crucial moment of truth came in 1962 when voters living in the district were presented with a bond issue referendum to finance the construction of BART. By this time the two northern counties of Marin and San Mateo had withdrawn for various reasons, leaving only San Francisco, Contra Costa, and Alameda counties. Needing a sixty percent favorable vote, the bond issue received approval by a slim one percent. This was accomplished despite strong opposition from the influential *San Francisco Chronicle*, which repeatedly denounced the project as extravagant and wasteful.

During the next ten years BART faced continued problems, including a time-consuming taxpayers' suit, large cost overruns, construction delays, and persistent funding problems. By 1968 BART faced its greatest crisis; out of funds and still far from completion of the construction phase, under incessant attack from critics of many different political persuasions, BART faced a grim future—if a future at all. At this crucial point, however, the California State Legislature investigated BART's financial problems, concluded that they were the result of technological upgrading of original plans and inflation, and authorized a district sales tax to cover the deficit.

With this strong support from the legislature, which itself was beginning to feel the brisk winds of public opposition to more freeways, BART now moved steadily ahead. Construction, which had actually begun in 1964, now moved into high gear. In sum, BART authorized 180 separate construction contracts at an initial cost of $825 million; the seventy-five mile system was about evenly divided between traditional ground-level, elevated, and underground track. The underground segments included the spectacular 3.6 mile underwater Trans-Bay Tube, a twin-bore tube that crossed under the bay from Oakland to San Francisco. This portion of the system alone cost $180 million, but it was the vital link in the entire system. Imaginative engineering design for the tube included fifty-seven prefabricated individual segments which were joined at the bottom of the bay. Each of the steel and concrete segments was forty-eight feet wide and twenty-seven feet high. Engineers from around the world praised the design; not only did it actually change direction eight times underwater, but even incorporated safety features to withstand possible earthquakes.

While construction moved steadily ahead, BART officials also devoted considerable attention to the system they hoped to have on line by 1971. The BART system, which serves thirty separate cities containing 2,500,000 people and covering 1,500 square miles, was designed to supplement the extensive freeway system to provide a balanced transportation system for the Bay Area. It was never intended to replace the automobile. Engineers designed BART to handle thirty thousand passengers during a normal work day. Early in its planning stages, BART officials agreed that in order to lure commuters from their private automobiles, BART would have to combine speed, luxury, convenience and economy. Thus the following objectives became part of the planning:

1. The electric-powered trains must be fast, with capability of speeds up to eighty miles per hour, with an average speed including station stops of forty miles per hour. Such speeds would cut in half average automobile commuter time.

2. The ride must be both comfortable and quiet, affording businessmen an environment in which to read and work on reports. The interior of the

cars thus featured carpeting, good acoustical qualities, pleasing decor, comfortable seating, and good ventilation.
3. Operational costs must be kept to a minimum in order to keep fares low. These plans included electronic computer safety monitoring devices and an automatic system of controlling the movement of the trains.
4. Environmental concerns, including the consumption of fuel and the noise level both inside and outside the trains, must receive special attention.

Throughout, emphasis was placed upon automation, and the outcome was an extraordinarily sophisticated control system which was capable of operating 105 separate trains simultaneously at seventy-five miles per hour. Electronic controls would monitor the entire system, adjusting individual train speeds to track conditions; they would even start and stop the trains automatically and open and close doors. Further, an automatic ticket purchase system would enable passengers to purchase reusable $20 tickets good for up to sixty separate trips; even the processing of the ticket would be done by electronic machines, automatically deducting the cost of the trip and imprinting upon the ticket the value remaining. Finally, each station was designed not only to provide efficient flow of passenger traffic, but also to insure a quiet and pleasant environment.

In September of 1972, BART finally began operations on a limited basis. Its opening had been delayed by many technological problems, as well as a crippling labor strike at the company holding the prime contract to build the attractive passenger cars. Shortly after commencing operation, a malfunctioning crystal in the central control system caused a derailment. Although no serious injuries resulted, BART had suffered a tremendous public relations setback. The derailed train only began a new series of frustrating problems for the system.

During its first year of operation, BART enjoyed at best very limited success. The $37 million control system has never worked satisfactorily; occasionally car doors open while the train is moving at seventy miles per hour, and officials have held up use of the Trans-Bay Tube pending additional safety checks. By early 1974, BART once more faced the possibility of going broke; it was already four years behind its operational schedule, and due to inflationary pressures as well as low estimates, had already exceeded its original budget by sixty percent. Technological problems were so large as to force the California Public Utilities Commission to halt tests upon its safety equipment until significant changes could be made. Yet, as one BART spokesman observed, "When you are the first transit system to be built in fifty years, and when you are attempting to stretch into the future to get the best technology available, you can expect bugs."[11]

When both its technological and financial problems are solved, BART will still only provide a partial solution to San Francisco's tremendous transit needs. The city's bus system needs rejuvenation, and its officials are frankly unable to find a means to arrest the continued loss of passengers. And even when BART is in full operation, the metropolis will still be heavily dependent upon the omnipresent automobile and its extensive freeway system. While

BART officials remain optimistic and are moving ahead with plans to incorporate Marin and San Mateo counties to the north by the mid-eighties, and eventually to make a grand loop around the bay to tie in San Jose as originally projected back in the early 1950s, the immediate and long-range prospects of the futuristic system remain clouded with complex problems.

The Future of Urban America

The immense difficulties of BART, however, were obscured in the 1970s by the sudden popularity of the concept of mass transit. To many it had become the new panacea for urban ills—not only would it reduce traffic congestion, help eliminate environmental pollution, and solve a long-standing urban transportation dilemma of the poor and elderly, but it would require much less fuel than is burned each day by the millions of automobiles that crowd the urban streets and freeways. Visionary transit enthusiasts told congressional committees and a suddenly interested public about cutting commuting time in half, about high-speed trains, which would be supplemented by computerized mini-buses in the central cities and the outlying suburban communities; they told of the end to automobile-produced air pollution. By 1974 multibillion dollar systems were already under construction in Washington, D.C., Baltimore, Atlanta, and Denver. And scores of other major cities were seriously considering similar projects.

Even the megalopolis that gave America the freeway was interested. Los Angeles, the city that had pointed the nation in the direction of "automobility," had become seriously afflicted by its own creation. The sprawling megalopolis had been carried to its immense size and power by the automobile, but now its leaders were having serious second thoughts about future freeway construction. The nation's most automobile-conscious metropolis, as journalist Harrison Salisbury put it, "lies nestled under its blanket of smog, girdled by bands of freeways, its core eviscerated by concrete strips and asphalt fields, its circulatory arteries pumping away without focus, the prototype of gasopolis, the rubber wheeled living region of the future." Nearly seven hundred miles of freeway were already in use, and with plans already prepared to build another eight hundred miles at a cost of in excess of $10 billion, city leaders began to question seriously additional concessions to the seemingly insatiable demands of the automobile.

Prodded by ever-darkening skies, fuel shortages, and the gloomy prospect of having to double its present seven hundred mile freeway system, Los Angeles County moved toward a 1975 referendum on a projected $8 billion transit system. Plans to include outlying Orange and San Bernadino Counties would move the total cost nearer to the $12 billion mark. The Southern California Rapid Transit District, popularly known by the ominous acronym of SCRTD, met with mild but apparently increasingly favorable public response. The idea of high-speed trains as an alternative to the jammed freeways began to spark enthusiasm among residents of the sprawling megalopolis. Providing the major stimulus was the city's energetic new mayor,

Tom Bradley. "We are at the point of history now where we have to stop saying, 'Can we build a total balanced transportation system for Los Angeles?' But rather, 'When do we start?' "[12]

It was in the midst of this popular movement toward urban transit that President Richard Nixon announced his massive new program in February of 1974 (*Alternatives 2 and 3*: see Document 13). This new thrust in federal policy had been emerging for several years, but now public opinion was ready (see Document 14). In 1973, for example, the Vice-President Spiro Agnew, himself later well known for close ties with highway contractors in Maryland, had told a Los Angeles audience that, "The automobile is not a monster, but it will become one if we allow ourselves to become totally dependent upon it for our urban transportation. We can develop more rational and efficient ways to move around in our cities, and mass transit—whether it be bus, rail or an innovative new system—can free us from our automobile servitude."[13]

Brave new thoughts for what was a self-proclaimed "conservative" Republican administration. And yet the panacea of mass transit remained nothing more than a hope and a dream. The older subway and commuter train systems in Chicago and New York City were still overwhelmed by the immensity of their task and the paucity of federal or state aid. Long ignored by federal policy, they were in need of massive financial aid merely to sustain operations. And in virtually every city, bus systems were deeply immersed in red ink and caught up in a continuing downward spiral of dwindling passenger usage and growing deficits. Their needs for government subsidy would be great, and unless federal funds would be forthcoming in large amounts, they would inevitably be forced to cease operations. And, despite the multimillion dollar futuristic systems like BART or SCRDT, transportation experts recognized that the less glamorous bus systems would prove to be the best solution for most cities.

Not only did the problems of finance remain to be solved. There also remained the powerful attractions afforded by the private automobile— gasoline shortage or no. The ominous threat to transit projects posed by the automobile was cogently summarized in 1974 by a parking attendant at a Long Beach restaurant: "It don't make all that much difference how many trains they put all around here. Maybe some dudes will ride them, but there'll be millions of them out there tied up in traffic but still grooving on their cars. I'm one of them: They'll have to take my car away from me to get me on a train."[14]

Fuel shortages, smog, congestion, inefficiency, appalling accident rates, spiralling insurance costs, immense environmental and social concerns, astronomical construction costs are all serious problems resulting from an overdependence upon the automobile. Yet if the outspoken youth in Long Beach was any indication of the underlying reaction to mass transit—and this author believes he was—then the future of mass transit as an alternative to the urban freeway and the automobile will be at best a difficult one, because the great American love affair with the automobile is still far from finished.

Notes

1. United States Bureau of the Census, *Preliminary Report*, 1970.

2. John Jerome, *The Death of the Automobile* (New York: Norton, 1972), p. 107.

3. Ibid., p. 108.

4. Kenneth Schneider, *Autokind vs. Mankind* (New York: Norton, 1971), p. 58.

5. Sam Bass Warner, Jr., *The Urban Wilderness* (New York: Harper & Row, 1972), pp. 47-48.

6. Robert Thruelson, "Coast to Coast Without Stopping," *Saturday Evening Post*, October 20, 1956, p. 65.

7. Alan Lupo, et al., *Rites of Way* (Boston: Little, Brown & Co., 1971), p. 106.

8. Juan Cameron, "How the Interstate Changed the Face of the Nation," *Fortune*, July, 1971, p. 81.

9. *Public Papers of Lyndon B. Johnson, 1963-64* (Washington, D.C.: Government Printing Office, 1965), vol. 1, p. 115.

10. Quoted in Cameron, "How the Interstate Changed the Face of the Nation," p. 125.

11. *The National Observer*, December 1, 1973, p. 19.

12. Ibid.

13. Associated Press News Service, March 21, 1973.

14. *The National Observer*, December 1, 1973, p. 19.

Part two

Documents of the Decision

1

Early Problems with Urban Expressways

California led the nation in the development of urban expressways. Even by the early 1950s, in microcosm, the first freeways pointed to the problems that would later become a national issue in the 1960s. In 1953, the executive director of the League of California Cities told his colleagues that an overreliance upon expressways would create serious problems. Already he noticed a serious problem for mass transit, and in a most perceptive commentary for the 1950s, raised a point central to urban transportation planning: "I question a transportation concept which seeks to assure every man an inalienable right to drive his vehicle alone to the central districts of our metropolitan areas and park" (*Alternative 2*). Thus, three years before the enactment of the Interstate program, a prominent California official had pointed directly at the problems that would surface in nearly every American metropolis by 1970.

Document†

We have been making transportation studies of metropolitan areas here in California for a very long time. Studies with which nothing has been done. I think that has happened because it is easier, both politically and in other ways, to build highways than it is to deal with the problems of mass transit. As a result we have neglected and largely destroyed our mass transit systems. This is not to suggest that we have enough freeways or enough highways, but I do mean to suggest that we don't have enough mass transit and that we must give attention to the need for an over-all, integrated system of transportation. There are those who say we have had enough study, what we need is action. I agree we need action, but I don't think we know where we are going. There are those who say that if we build freeways we will have solved the problem of transit. If anybody really said that—it is ridiculous. We are now, in this session of the legislature, on the threshold, I hope, of action which will greatly accelerate the rate of highway construction in our State. This is highly desirable and necessary. I propose to fight for it along with others who so strongly believe that we must have a greatly accelerated

†From: Richard Graves, "California's Urban Transportation Problem," *Urban Transportation*, February, 1953, pp. 83-84.

program. But if we do not at the same time, and as a part of the same program, deal with the same determination and vigor with the need for mass transit within these metropolitan areas—giving thoughtful reexamination to our transportation needs and requirements—we will defeat the purposes of our highway program.

I have only recently become an expert on transit, I think I have attended two meetings and made three speeches. But there are some things that are perfectly evident, even to the specialist in generalities like me and to the average interested citizen. There is one thing that a freeway can do, without question: It can divert and generate enough traffic to make it your most congested road the day it is opened and from then on. But there is certainly a question where this single-minded concentration on the metropolitan freeway as the single method of moving people and goods from here to there offers, standing alone, any solution at all to the problem of transportation. I question very much whether there is enough money in the world to build that many freeways. I question very much whether we can remove that much land and property from our tax rolls, not only for freeway rights-of-way, but also for the parking space which would be required. I question a transportation concept which seeks to assure every man an inalienable right to drive his vehicle alone to the central districts of our metropolitan areas and park.

About a year and a half ago, the League of California Cities started asking the legislative joint interim committee to take a good long look at the major highway problems of the metropolitan areas along with the state highway problems in those metropolitan areas. We wanted to start building up a factual foundation upon which to measure not only what our highway problem is but also what our over-all transportation problem is. This we never yet have been able to do. Some of the information has, however, been gathered by the public-works officers, and management people of the metropolitan centers and will be supplied to the interim committee. The research has not been as thorough as we had hoped for. And so, in recognition of our inability to deal with the problem through this machinery we proposed at the August special session of the Legislature a resolution, authored by Assemblyman H. Allen Smith of Glendale, which called upon the Institute of Transportation and Traffic Engineering at the University to tell the legislature in March of this year what would be involved in a real study of the total transportation problems of our metropolitan areas. The resolution was adopted and Mr. Davis and his associates have since been preparing this—not a piece of research—but a prospectus for research. It will be submitted to the legislature shortly. This session we requested Assemblyman Smith, in pursuance of this earlier resolution, to introduce a bill appropriating—an arbitrary figure to get everyone's sight on the right dimension—a million dollars to carry out the studies which will be suggested by the prospectus.

There are a lot of bills in the Legislature asking for State money for research. A good many of them are concerned solely with transit, that is, mass transit. But at least one, in addition to our own, says transit and traffic,

which I infer covers the idea of transportation. These bills range from
$400,000 to $1 million. The question is, first, should we deal with studies of
highways separately from studies of transit leaving it to the good will of men
to get together and achieve a coordinated, integrated result? Or should be
provide within the legislation itself the absolute means of coordinated
research by dealing with it as a single problem? Well, I have never yet seen
men cooperate in a coordinated research effort when their personal or
vocational interests were so vitally affected. I think it is absolutely essential
that if any research is to be done—and it must be—then it should be research
in transportation as a total problem of movement of people and goods within
a metropolitan environment, and that we should come up with a single,
coordinated, integrated plan. I submit that we have backed into this one by
going so far with our highway and freeway planning while we have done
nothing about mass-transit planning. At the risk of offending my friends who
are interested primarily in highways let me say that, so far as my relatively
uninformed opinion is concerned, I should think the movement of people in
the metropolitan areas proceeds from mass transit, and to make it even more
specific, rail rapid transit. In those specific situations where population
densities are concentrated it seems to me that rail rapid transit is and has to
be, not a supplement but the basic form of transportation, to be
appropriately supplemented by other forms of mass transit such as the bus. It
seems to me that we should use highways and freeways for the purpose for
which they are and ought to be designed within the larger framework of
transportation. I could be wrong about these things. I am not an expert, and I
look at it only as a student of local government, attempting to see the
inter-relationships of things.

One of the greatest problems which concerns us now in cities, both the
small ones and the larger ones, and from one end of the state to the other, is
the problem of urban sprawl—this uncoordinated, unplanned, unreasoned,
and uneconomic spreadingout of the metropolitan areas by a series of private
decisions on the part of speculators and developers and the like. They are
privileged to operate as a free enterprise, but they do not have the right as a
result of their private decisions to impose impossible and prohibitively
expensive problems on the whole community. We are concerned about urban
sprawl for several reasons, but it is a large factor in the problem of
transportation. If we are going to have a well conceived transportation plan
we must also begin to look at regulating land use and development so that the
two are in some respects at least consistent. It is not amusing when some of
the very cities which are concerned about their sprawling fringes want to
develop highways and freeways which will give unlimited encouragement to
the very decentralization which they say is tearing their guts out. And yet it is
the facility of transportation which has and will decentralize our cities. I am
not saying they shouldn't be decentralized, I only say we ought to know what
we are doing when we do it, and we do not.

Now all this argues that nothing should be done until we do some more
research. Nothing could be farther from my purpose. But I do contend that

we should do only those things now, and as quickly as we can, that reasonable men can agree should be done in any event. Some matters are so obvious and the pattern is so fixed that as to those things at least there will be no great change regardless of what research may indicate. By and large, this is true of the mainline state highway system within metropolitan areas and it is largely true of the mainline system throughout the state.

There is no reason why we should not get as much money as can be justified to build the mainline state highway system as fast as we can build it, with due regard for economics of construction. We ought to do that. We are urging that it be done, and there is in this proposal for concurrent research no necessity for delay in the construction of the primary system and the freeways which are a part of it, inside and outside the metropolitan areas. If we could build the system in ten years we should do it, if it can be justified in engineering and economic terms. . . .

2

Eisenhower's Message to Congress, 1955

The driving force behind the establishment of the Interstate system was President Eisenhower. Beginning in early 1954 he pushed hard to establish such a system, and during the summer of that year he appointed a special advisory committee headed by General Lucius Clay. Upon receiving the Clay committee's report in early 1955, Eisenhower sent a major highway message to the Congress. A central point of his message was that he endorsed the Trust Fund concept (*Alternative 1*). Even with the president's strong support, however, political issues prevented Congress from taking action for more than a year. Readers will note with interest that President Eisenhower sees no relationship between the Interstate and other systems of urban transportation.

Document†

To the Congress of the United States:

Our unity as a nation is sustained by free communication of thought and by easy transportation of people and goods. The ceaseless flow of information throughout the Republic is matched by individual and commercial movement over a vast system of interconnected highways criss-crossing the Country and joining at our national borders with friendly neighbors to the north and south.

Together, the uniting forces of our communication and transportation systems are dynamic elements in the very name we bear—United States. Without them, we would be a mere alliance of many separate parts.

The Nation's highway system is a gigantic enterprise, one of our largest items of capital investment. Generations have gone into its building. Three million, three hundred and sixty-six thousand miles of road, travelled by 58 million motor vehicles, comprise it. The replacement cost of its drainage and bridge and tunnel works is incalculable. One in every seven Americans gains his livelihood and supports his family out of it. But, in large part, the network is inadequate for the nation's growing needs.

†From: Dwight D. Eisenhower, "Special Message to the Congress Regarding a National Highway Program," February 22, 1955, *Public Papers of the Presidents, Dwight D. Eisenhower, 1955* (Washington, D.C.: Government Printing Office, 1959), pp. 275-80.

In recognition of this, the Governors in July of last year at my request began a study of both the problem and methods by which the Federal Government might assist the States in its solution. I appointed in September the President's Advisory Committee on a National Highway Program, headed by Lucius D. Clay, to work with the Governors and to propose a plan of action for submission to the Congress. At the same time, a committee representing departments and agencies of the national Government was organized to conduct studies coordinated with the other two groups.

All three were confronted with inescapable evidence that action, comprehensive and quick and forward-looking, is needed.

First: Each year, more than 36 thousand people are killed and more than a million injured on the highways. To the home where the tragic aftermath of an accident on an unsafe road is a gap in the family circle, the monetary worth of preventing that death cannot be reckoned. But reliable estimates place the measurable economic cost of the highway accident toll to the Nation at more than $4.3 billion a year.

Second: The physical condition of the present road net increases the cost of vehicle operation, according to many estimates, by as much as one cent per mile of vehicle travel. At the present rate of travel, this totals more than $5 billion a year. The cost is not borne by the individual vehicle operator alone. It pyramids into higher expense of doing the nation's business. Increased highway transportation costs, passed on through each step in the distribution of goods, are paid ultimately by the individual consumer.

Third: In case of an atomic attack on our key cities, the road net must permit quick evacuation of target areas, mobilization of defense forces and maintenance of every essential economic function. But the present system in critical areas would be the breeder of a deadly congestion within hours of an attack.

Fourth: Our Gross National Product, about $357 billion in 1954, is estimated to reach over $500 billion in 1965 when our population will exceed 180 million and, according to other estimates, will travel in 81 million vehicles 814 billion vehicle miles that year. Unless the present rate of highway improvement and development is increased, existing traffic jams only faintly foreshadow those of ten years hence.

To correct these deficiencies is an obligation of Government at every level. The highway system is a public enterprise. As the owner and operator, the various levels of Government have a responsibility for management that promotes the economy of the nation and properly serves the individual user. In the case of the Federal Government, moreover, expenditures on a highway program are a return to the highway user of the taxes which he pays in connection with his use of the highways.

Congress has recognized the national interest in the principal roads by authorizing two Federal-aid systems, selected cooperatively by the States, local units and the Bureau of Public Roads.

The Federal-aid primary system as of July 1, 1954, consisted of 234,407 miles, connecting all the principal cities, county seats, ports, manufacturing areas and other traffic generating centers.

In 1944 the Congress approved the Federal-aid secondary system, which on July 1, 1954, totalled 482,972 miles, referred to as farm-to-market roads—important feeders linking farms, factories, distribution outlets and smaller communities with the primary system.

Because some sections of the primary system, from the viewpoint of national interest are more important than others, the Congress in 1944 authorized the selection of a special network, net to exceed 40,000 miles in length, which would connect by routes, as direct as practicable, the principal metropolitan areas, cities and industrial centers, serve the national defense, and connect with routes of continental importance in the Dominion of Canada and the Republic of Mexico.

This National System of Interstate Highways, although it embraces only 1.2 percent of total road mileage, joins 42 State capital cities and 90 percent of the urban and 45 percent of the rural population. Approximately 37,600 miles have been designated to date. This system and its mileage are presently included within the Federal-aid primary system.

In addition to these systems, the Federal Government has the principal, and in many cases the sole, responsibility for roads that cross or provide access to Federally owned land—more than one-fifth the nation's area.

Of all these, the Interstate System must be given top priority in construction planning. But at the current rate of development, the Interstate network would not reach even a reasonable level of extent and efficiency in half a century. State highway departments cannot effectively meet the need. Adequate right-of-way to assure control of access; grade separation structures; relocation and realignment of present highways; all these, done on the necessary scale within an integrated system, exceed their collective capacity.

If we have a congested and unsafe and inadequate system, how then can we improve it so that ten years from now it will be fitted to the nation's requirements?

A realistic answer must be based on a study of all phases of highway financing, including a study of the costs of completing the several systems of highways, made by the Bureau of Public Roads in cooperation with the State highway departments and local units of government. This study, made at the direction of the 83rd Congress in the 1954 Federal-aid Highway Act, is the most comprehensive of its kind ever undertaken.

Its estimates of need show that a 10-year construction program to modernize all our roads and streets will require expenditure of $101 billion by all levels of Government.

The preliminary 10-year totals of needs by road systems are:

Billions

Interstate (urban $11, rural $12 billion)..$ 23
Federal-aid Primary (urban $10, rural $20 billion) 30
Federal-aid Secondary (entirely rural) 15

Sub-total of Federal-aid Systems (urban $21, rural $47 billion)........... 68
Other roads and streets (urban $16, rural $17 billion)............................... 33

Total of needs (urban $37, rural $64 billion).......................................$101

The Governors' Conference and the President's Advisory Committee are agreed that the Federal share of the needed construction program should be about 30 percent of the total, leaving to State and local units responsibility to finance the remainder.

The obvious responsibility to be accepted by the Federal Government, in addition to the existing Federal interest in our 3,366,000-mile network of highways, is the development of the Interstate System with its most essential urban arterial connections.

In its report, the Advisory Committee recommends:

1. That the Federal Government assume principal responsibility for the cost of a modern Interstate Network to be completed by 1964 to include the most essential urban arterial connections; at an annual average cost of $2.5 billion for the ten year period.
2. That Federal contributions to primary and secondary road systems, now at the rate authorized by the 1954 Act of approximately $525 million annually, be continued.
3. That Federal funds for that portion of the Federal-aid systems in urban areas not on the Interstate System, now approximately $75 million annually, be continued.
4. That Federal funds for Forest Highways be continued at the present $22.5 million per year rate.

Under these proposals, the total Federal expenditures through the ten year period would be:

Billions

Interstate System...$25.000
Federal-aid Primary and Secondary... 5.250
Federal-aid Urban .... .750
Forest Highways .... .225

Total $31.225

The extension of necessary highways in the Territories and highway maintenance and improvement in National Parks, on Indian lands and on other public lands of the United States will continue to be treated in the budget for these particular subjects.

A sound Federal highway program, I believe, can and should stand on its own feet, with highway users providing the total dollars necessary for improvement and new construction. Financing of interstate and Federal-aid systems should be based on the planned use of increasing revenues from present gas and diesel oil taxes, augmented in limited instances with tolls.

I am inclined to the view that it is sounder to finance this program by special bond issues, to be paid off by the above-mentioned revenues which will be collected during the useful life of the roads and pledged to this purpose, rather than by an increase in general revenue obligations.

At this time, I am forwarding for use by the Congress in its deliberations the Report to the President made by the President's Advisory Committee on a National Highway Program. This study of the entire highway traffic problem and presentation of a detailed solution for its remedy is an analytical review of the major elements in a most complex situation. In addition, the Congress will have available the study made by the Bureau of Public Roads at the direction of the 83rd Congress.

These two documents together constitute a most exhaustive examination of the National highway system, its problems and their remedies. Inescapably, the vastness of the highway enterprise fosters varieties of proposals which must be resolved into a national highway pattern. The two reports, however, should generate recognition of the urgency that presses upon us; approval of a general program that will give us a modern safe highway system; realization of the rewards for prompt and comprehensive action. They provide a solid foundation for a sound program.

DWIGHT D. EISENHOWER

3 ══════════

══════════ Public
Hearings on a
National
Highway
Program

The President's Advisory Committee on a National Highway Program held public hearings on October 7-8, 1954. The groups that were permitted to present testimony constitutes a good sampling of the diversity of membership of the "Highway Lobby." An intraadministration memorandum cogently summarized the testimony of the various groups. The complete statements together with various types of supporting documents may be found at the Eisenhower Library in Abilene, in the committee files. Special attention is called to the summary of the testimony by Robert Moses on behalf of the U. S. Conference of Mayors.

Document†

Bureau of Public Roads

October 11, 1954

Mr. A. C. Clark
H. A. Radzikowski
Summary of Clay Committee Hearings—October 7 and 8, 1954
General L. Clay. Called attention to $101.3 billion highway construction requirements for next 10 years, $54.5 billion deficit in financing, and expressed a favorable attitude for an enlarged road program.
American Farm Bureau Federation. President's proposal for an additional $50 billion for highways should be scaled down. Terminate Federal gas tax and reduce percentage of Federal highway participation. Recognize States' rights. No allocation of Federal funds for toll roads.
U. S. Chamber of Commerce. Favors Federal-aid highway principle. Not ready to make recommendations on President's $50 billion program. Their special studies and regional public meetings on subject will not be completed until January 1955.
U. S. Conference of Mayors, by Robert Moses. We need at least $50 billion in next 10 years for highways, including $15 billion in metropolitan

†From: "Summary of Clay Committee Hearings—October 7 and 8, 1954," John S. Bragdon Files, Eisenhower Library, Abilene, Kansas.

areas. Cities are deep in traffic trouble. City highway construction costs from $1 to $15 million a mile. Off-street parking and coordination with slum clearance also needed. Local pressures should be overcome by Federal Government establishing engineering standards which can only be departed from by loss of Federal aid. Will later confer with committee on further suggestions.

American Road Builders' Association. Agrees with President's proposed program. Advocates continuing present Federal grants-in-aid through present established procedures. Supplement with Federal credits for expanding program including toll roads. Federal Government should take greater responsibility for interstate system. Determine abilities and facilities of the various segments of the highway industry to carry out such a program in an economical and efficient manner.

National Association of County Officials. Counties will not be able to and will not seek participation in increased $50 billion program. They are under legal and practical restrictions to raise contributing funds. Urges that when focusing attention on interstate and primary systems, State funds should not be so committed that counties would lose part of their share of State gas tax.

Automotive Safety Foundation. Their engineers confirm estimates of $101 billion highway needs except on interstate system. Bureau of Public Roads increased interstate standards somewhat higher than used in the past to measure needs on that system. Obsolete State Laws are a bottleneck, especially on right-of-way to provide limited access.

American Automobile Association. Reappraising policy in view of President's proposal and will not have recommendations until Detroit convention in 2 weeks. Interstate system regarded as most important and endorse past action of Congress increasing Federal share of participation. Controlled access is absolutely essential. Greatest economic loss in deficient urban highways and terminal facilities.

Associated General Contractors. President's proposal is realistic. Construction costs are down and full value can be received on new program. Contractors have the capacity and keen competition exists for work. Can double capacity in 2 years. Shortage of engineers, inadequate right-of-way laws and possible local shortage of some materials could be bottlenecks. Highways should be completed between principal points of travel instead of a few spot miles. That's what makes toll roads popular.

American Petroleum Institute. Shocked at new estimate of $101 billion increase by Bureau of Public Roads from $55 billion in 2 months. Criticized limited access provisions of Interstate Policy Memorandum No. 20-4, also Bureau of Public Roads' proposal to relocate 90 percent of interstate system. This is an attempt to effect a radical and serious up-grading of standards. It directly, adversely, and seriously affects many thousands of businessmen who depend upon these highways as their market place. Contrary to traditional free enterprise.

Highway Municipal Association. Federal Government should concentrate effort on interstate system. Cities are most critical area and Federal highway laws recognize it. More than half of Federal gas tax is earned on city streets. Favor long-term Federal financing on a 60 Federal-40 State ratio for all new work. State to sell bonds and Federal Government to pledge retirement of its share yearly. Federal Government should set up financing authority.

Truck-Trailer Manufacturers Association. Federal Government should make grants of aid based on need of city exit facilities as a national defense measure. Greater responsibility of Federal Government on interstate system is favored and increased Federal financing. Other roads are local responsibility. Third structure highway-user tax opposed.

Independent Advisory Committee to the Trucking Industry, Inc. (David Beck of AFL Teamsters Union is a member of this Committee.) Favors increased road program. Should correlate with civil defense needs. Roads so crowded because of increased rate of passenger car production that in one State there is agitation to ban trucks from highways on weekends. Federal Government should finance highways like any other defense measure.

American Association of State Highway Officials. Read W.A.S.H.O. and S.A.S.H.O. Resolutions recommending $2 billion, 100 percent annual Federal bond financing of interstate system. Continue same Federal-aid policy on other systems. Limited access needed on interstate system and Federal eminent domain to expedite. Highway industry capacity is $5 billion and can step up to $9 billion in 5 years. In financing program there should be no linkage between gas tax and Federal obligation to build roads. Difference between $50 billion and $101 billion deficiency estimate is due to old estimate being based on current deficiencies and new estimate 10 years from now on 1974 traffic requirements. Also, Bureau of Public Roads used interstate standards. A.A.S.H.O. must first meet in convention in November 1954 before spelling out policy for President's additional $50 billion highway program.

Association of American Railroads. Railroads favor good roads but favor truck transportation paying a larger share of the cost. Ask that highways assume a greater share of grade crossing elimination costs. Highway responsibility should remain in States. Toll roads should be fully self-supporting. Federal-aid should be curtailed. If not, a Federal highway-user (weight-distance) tax should be developed. Federal Government should lend, not give, money to local authorities. Federal aid should be used to operate weighing stations.

Private Truck Council of America. They doubt the need for $101 billion in 10 years. They believe need is nearer $50 billion. Want good roads but not a wasteful or excessive program. Eliminate all highway-user taxes except registration and motor fuel. Federal Government should repeal excise taxes. Suggests that present highway construction program is adequate.

American Trucking Association, by John V. Lawrence, Manager-Director. He is "running scared" in view of "astronomical" estimate of $54 billion more for highways in next 10 years. Recommend continuation of present primary, secondary, and urban Federal-aid procedures and that Federal Government assume full financing of interstate system. Recommend expenditure of $2 billion a year for 10 years on interstate system. Third structure taxes such as "ton-mile" set up "Chinese Walls" at State lines to impede interstate commerce.

Toll Roads Association. They asked to testify, were not invited. Stated that 90 percent of traffic desires to go around cities and not into them (this is almost exact opposite of our information, especially in regard to large cities). Asked that toll financing be used wherever possible.

The National Grange. Delegates have not yet met and they are not certain they will support President's increased $50 billion highway program. They support PAR movement and sufficiency rating highways. Our roads have been neglected during war years, they cause economic waste, and there is great need for improvement. Highway improvements should be used to stimulate economy and cut unemployment when needed. Membership would oppose program if it increased price of roadbuilding material or caused inefficient construction. New program would annually cost $94 per vehicle on road. Support present ratio of 45-30-35 Federal-aid distribution on various Federal-aid systems. Bond financing might be necessary.

National Association of Motor Bus Operators. Size of program dependent in part on capabilities of highway industry—supplies of construction machinery, materials, labor, and, particularly, trained highway engineers and supervisory personnel. Federal aid should be heavily concentrated upon interstate system: $2 billion per year for 10 years for this purpose merits serious consideration. This would release State funds for State highway responsibilities. Federal aid for other systems should be reduced correspondingly. Federal funds should be raised by taxes on broad base and not by levies on special groups. Federal Government must restrict aid program to financing highways essential to proper Federal functions. Favors Federal guarantee of bonds issued by State to finance work. Interstate system should be free of toll facilities.

4

A Voice
for Urban
Mass Transit

When the Clay committee held public hearings on a proposed new highway system, it issued invitations almost exclusively to those interested parties that would support a massive highway construction program. Among the groups that were excluded was the American Transit Association (ATA), the national organization that served as the spokesmen for urban transit systems in the United States. Several weeks after the committee ended its hearings, its executive vice-president submitted a letter to present the views of the ATA to the committee. Not only did the committee snub the ATA by not receiving its testimony along with the many prohighway groups, but the internal handling of the letter upon its receipt indicates that the committee members did not read the letter that is reprinted below.

Document†

Having noted that an opportunity has recently been accorded the American Trucking Associations, Inc., the National Association of Motor Bus Operators, the American Automobile Association, and other highway users to submit statements on national highway matters on behalf of their respective industries, we respectfully submit a statement on behalf of the urban transit industry of the United States, which the American Transit Association represents to the extent of more than 80 percent of the volume of passenger business handled, and on behalf of the millions of American citizens who, through choice or necessity make regular use of this means of transportation. Membership in the American Transit Association also is representative of both publicly- and privately-owned transit systems.

An efficient and healthy local transit industry in the urban and suburban areas of the country, comprising street car, trolley coach and motor bus operations, as well as elevated and subway rapid transit lines, is of extreme importance to the general well-being of our Nation. The full importance of the transit industry to national defense was well demonstrated during World War II, when operating transit companies were called upon to carry an unprecedented volume of people when curtailment in use of the private automobile became necessary in the face of shortages of rubber and motor fuel.

In the peak year of 1945, the transit industry handled twenty-three and a

---

†From: George W. Anderson to President's Advisory Committee on a National Highway Program, October 25, 1954, Eisenhower Papers, Eisenhower Library.

quarter billion riders and, in spite of the widespread post-war use of the private automobile, still carried fourteen billion riders during the year 1953. In the larger cities, such as New York and Philadelphia, as much as 80% of the people entering and leaving the central business districts do so by public transit, with the percentage approaching 60% in other cities of which Atlanta, Georgia, and Kansas City, Mo., are examples.

We in the local transit industry are quite cognizant of the need for a modern and efficient interstate and intercity network of highways. However, we also are aware that the problem of traffic congestion—the limiting factor on traffic movement—is much more a problem of the urban areas than that of the intercity or interstate highway systems. Thus, we urge that much greater consideration be given to how assistance under a national highway program can be given to local communities in their efforts to combat the tremendous delays and economic losses resulting from urban traffic congestion so that, in turn, maximum returns in benefits to the entire national highway transportation setup can be obtained.

Much emphasis has been put upon the construction of freeways or expressways through and into urban areas in order that increasingly greater numbers of private automobiles may have increasingly greater freedom of movement. Sight is lost of the fact, however, that as these expressways and freeways feed more and more automobiles into already congested urban districts the problem of traffic congestion becomes more acute. This constantly sharpening terminal problem involves street facilities for the distribution of the greater volumes of traffic induced by freeway construction, and creates a demand for constantly enlarged off-street parking facilities, the combined effect being an ever-increasing drain upon our national economy for the provision of facilities for the primary use of the private motorist.

Even the most ardent advocates of the use of the private passenger automobile now recognize that it will never be possible to move all of the people into and out of central business districts who may desire to use that medium of transportation. Urban street systems, and present and prospective off-street parking facilities, never will be able to absorb that volume. There will have to be continuing dependence upon public transit facilities if the central business districts of our cities are to survive and prosper. This fact now has been recognized by downtown merchants, real estate interests, and municipal regulatory and taxing authorities, who are making efforts to gain further and more general recognition of the urban traffic problem. It is important, therefore, that in any expenditure of funds by the Federal government for improved national highway transportation, the urban and suburban areas with their systems of public transit not be overlooked. Appropriate consideration must be given to facilitating the movement of public transit passengers as well as to facilitating the movement of persons in private automobiles.

The urban transit industry merits such consideration because it is a taxpayer. Of greater importance, however, is the fact that the transit vehicle is a much more efficient instrument for the movement of people than is the private automobile. Since the urban-suburban problem is primarily one of moving people and goods rather than one of moving vehicles, this factor should not be overlooked. The following examples serve to illustrate this point:

A transit route operated with 50-seat motor buses or trolley coaches on a 30-second headway can move 6,720 riders per hour one way. It would require 4,480 automobiles to carry this same number of passengers at prevailing peak occupancy ratios, and these autos would require three (3) one-way traffic lanes for their movement, the equivalent of 1.5 four-lane expressways.

A transit route operated with 60-seat street cars on a 30-second headway can move 9,600 riders per hour one way. It would require 6,400 automobiles to carry this same number of passengers at prevailing peak occupancy ratios, and these autos would require 4.3 one-way traffic lanes for their movement, the equivalent of more than two four-lane expressways.

The operation of street cars in three-car trains one minute apart would provide for the movement of 14,400 riders per hour. It would require 9,600 automobiles to carry this same number of passengers, and these autos would require 6.4 one-way traffic lanes for their movement, the equivalent of more than three four-lane expressways.

A rapid transit train of modest dimensions operated on 1½ minute intervals can handle 48,000 riders per hour one way. It would require 32,000 autos to carry this same number of passengers, and these autos would in turn require 21.3 one-way traffic lanes for their movement, the equivalent of more than 10 four-lane expressways.

Most significant of all, perhaps, from the standpoint of the urban economy is the fact that none of these transit passengers require parking space either on- or off-street when they arrive in the central business district.

Thus, if provisions were made on expressways entering or passing through central business districts for the inclusion of high-speed express transit services, either rail or rubber-tired, the dimensions of these very expensive expressway facilities would be greatly reduced under those required for movement by private automobile alone. Such provisions for express-type transit operations can be made for a very small portion of the resulting total project cost. This is being well illustrated currently by the inclusion of a center mall for rail rapid transit facilities in the Congress Street Expressway in Chicago, where the additional right-of-way width was provided for an additional cost of approximately $150,000 per mile in a project with a total cost of one-hundred million dollars for eight miles. This does not include the cost of the transit facilities themselves, but the time may be approaching when governmental agencies will give consideration to the provision of roadway structures, platforms, stations and signal systems at public expense as part of their contributions to improved highway passenger transportation in order to avoid the tremendous expense and physical limitations to doing this job solely by means of the passenger automobile. This already has been done in some instances where turnouts and other facilities have been provided for express transit operations with motor buses.

In addition to the foregoing, there is an important correlation between the provision of adequate facilities for express transit operations and meeting the needs of rural groups, particularly farmers, for adequate highway transportation. By using transit in an effort to improve the efficiency of the expenditure of funds for the more expeditious movement of people in and around urban areas, there will be that much more money available with which to assist the farmers by meeting their needs for more extensive and better farm-to-market roads. Since there is a definite limit to the amount of money that can be spent for improving our highway transportation without seriously affecting the national economy, this consideration appears to be a most important one.

Still another consideration in connection with the use of funds on a national highway program is the urgent need for more extensive research in the fields of urban transportation as evidenced by considerations now before the National Research Council and the new program just getting under way with the sponsorship of the recently organized National Committee on Urban Transportation. The U.S. Bureau of Public Roads, which has done much able work in the past, is among the groups anxious to see more attention given to the needs of urban areas, to the periodic gathering of pertinent factual information, and to the long-range planning for proper integration of all forms of transportation in urban areas.

Finally, appropriate balance in the allocation of funds would seem to indicate that consideration could be given to more extensive research in the field of highway traffic safety, where much still needs to be learned about the basic causes of accidents, safety in street and highway design, safety in vehicle design, and safety and efficiency in operational control.

We trust that you will find this statement on behalf of the urban transit industry of interest and value to the work of your Committee, and we will gladly offer any further assistance which we may be in a position to render. For the use of your Committee, we enclose 12 copies of this letter.

5

The Politics of Highways

Historians, for some inexplicable reasons, have devoted relatively little attention to the role of the automobile and highway policy as an integral part of American politics. In 1973, however, a doctoral candidate at the Ohio State University presented a dissertation that attempted to relate federal highway policy to the broader themes of American political and social history. Mark Rose's "Express Highway Politics, 1939-1956," provides a useful analysis of this relationship, and the concluding chapters of the study are of especial relevance to this book. Dr. Rose's observations help place into historical perspective the overriding significance of the creation of the Interstate system; that the real tragedy, from the point of view of the necessity of a balanced urban transportation system, is aptly summarized in Dr. Rose's first sentence: "The Interstate Highway Act foreclosed most of the options in American road politics."

Document†

The Interstate Highway Act foreclosed most of the options in American road politics. For the next decade or so, engineers and users were preoccupied with completing the Interstate System rapidly, free from political squabbles about allocation formulas and the distribution of power. Yet debate and conflict proceeded along anyhow, sometimes repeating old themes ritualistically.

Highway spending was largely inflexible under the 1956 Act. Nonetheless, members of the Council of Economic Advisers [CEA] were still seeking some method of varying the pace of road expenditures, hoping to develop another counter-cyclical weapon for the administration. They recognized that it would prove difficult to modify the Interstate Act. As Bragdon saw it, "the horse ... [was] out of the stable ...." After some indecisiveness initially, however, they fixed on the idea of advancing an amendment allowing deficit finance in the event of recessions and limiting road spending under inflationary conditions. If that tactic failed, they looked forward to reviewing financing procedures during a more general examination of road finance scheduled for 1959. On the other hand, Chairman Burns was not concerned with the political feasibility of CEA proposals, just "their technical and administrative soundness." In any case, none of their initiatives were successful.

The picture was much the same in terms of utilizing Interstate roads for

†From: Mark Howard Rose, "Express Highway Politics, 1939-1956" (Ph.D. dissertation, Ohio State University, 1973).

urban redevelopment purposes. Since BPR and state road engineers enjoyed control of the program, they had few incentives to include urban renewal and broader transportation objectives in their programming. As in the past, they defined their task as one of promoting traffic efficiency, not rebuilding cities or regenerating the urban social structure. While the 1962 Highway Act provided for consideration of urban transport and the city as a whole, engineers were able to maneuver their way around it adroitly, building roads largely as they wished. Only where urban leaders were committed to a unified program of renewal and mass transit were expressways built as part of some wider plan. Basically, then, the construction of the Interstate System followed the lines determined by highway users and road engineers.

Actually post-1956 highway politics was only a scaled down version of traditional patterns of political conflict within the road construction and urban rebuilding fields. Political conflict had been a part of highway construction for years. Certainly participants shared a number of values. They celebrated low taxes, balanced budgets and traffic efficiency as well as the more general goal of local autonomy. As a rule, too, they believed that more roads were vital to economic growth and, at some point, social harmony. While all this seemed right in principle, highway politics had been deadlocked since the depression, leaving the pace of road construction well-behind the huge upsurge in motor vehicles.

Factors largely outside of personal control such as inflation limited road mileage somewhat, but the real problems were social and political in nature. Diverse professional and commercial experiences shaped vastly different perspectives on highway traffic and urban problems. Road users and highway engineers always affirmed a benefit theory of taxation and endorsed highway construction which served traffic needs alone. In practice, these views meant that users would finance state roads through gasoline taxes, leaving the federal government to pay for national highways as part of its national defense and general welfare obligations. Whatever the theory, users and their allies did not intend to construct roads as part of some larger urban complex. As in the late 1930's, they claimed that roads were built for commerce.

Members of three presidential administrations shared many of these goals and values, supporting accelerated Interstate construction without much reference to general transportation and urban objectives. Yet they were at odds with engineers and users, largely over the level of federal financing. Essentially they wanted to vary the rate of road construction according to a wider understanding of economic needs. Through 1954 or so, they argued in favor of a relatively low level of road expenditures, trying to restrain inflationary movements. About a year through the first Eisenhower Administration, however, they reverted to advocating accelerated road construction, hoping to bolster the economy and relieve traffic congestion as well. Road users and their allies liked government road spending, but wanted a program which was free of taxes, more stable and subject to local control. In this sense, anyway, members of the Eisenhower team continued a practice begun under President Hoover.

Advocates of city remodeling and wider transportation planning composed another element in expressway politics. While they accepted the norms of traffic efficiency and were enthusiastic proponents of economic growth, they hoped to channel development according to notions of wider social utility. They believed that expressway construction should assist with local renewal projects and serve as one member of a larger urban transportation facility. Occasionally they spoke of expressways as part of a planned system of urban and rural communities. In any event, planners were the least successful group in road politics, winning only limited gains in a few cities. For that matter, their elaborate plans for remodeling the nation's transport system found little support at the federal or urban levels.

The Interstate Highway Act emerged from this milieu. But it did not represent a marked departure from the basic pattern of highway politics. While the Act was unique in many respects, it continued a number of traditional practices and grew from the very framework of highway affairs. By the mid-1950's traffic congestion seemed intolerable to most Americans. More important, truckers relented in their campaign to drop the federal gasoline tax. They were willing to finance the federal road system provided tax increases were moderate and ungraduated and all of the money was channeled into road construction. Finally, President Eisenhower's support for a program of accelerated road construction was vital for pushing the appropriate legislation through C ngress. In general, he assumed a national view of highway affairs, putting th economy prior to the immediate needs of road users. In this sense, he continued the practices of Presidents Truman and Roosevelt. But Eisenhower had to operate in a context of intolerable traffic and a receding economy. An accelerated road construction program promised to free traffic. If it was financed prudently, it also would hitch the economy to a gigantic public works project, capable of modifying the range of economic swings.

By early 1955, therefore, all of the political elements for a stepped up road program were in order. Although participants in road politics did not recognize it, they had settled most of the outstanding questions. Essentially they lost road legislation in 1955 because of differences over the details of finance and a high-level of commitment to certain principles. By 1956, their principles were dissolved by the press for more roads and a bill which asked few sacrifices, especially from users. Ultimately the Interstate Highway Act of 1956 embodied standard building and financing arrangements, incorporating techniques which had been used in the states for many years. In other cases, the Interstate Act brought to fruition the most basic aspirations of users, road engineers and three Presidents.

What emerged from this conflict was more expressways pure and simple. Builders did not have to consult with economists or the prcponents of social and physical planning. Nonetheless, there were alternatives available to this narrow form of highway construction. As far back as the late 1920's, there had been talk of greenbelt communities surrounded by fast-moving expressways. The General Motors' exhibit at the New York World's Fair in

1939 capped this trend of thought, promising regenerated cities and a traffic utopia. Then, too, there were all sorts of proposals for expressways which would contribute to an overhaul of the nation's transportation system and promote full employment. Later on, concern for full employment switched to planning for road building as one phase of a government effort to promote stable economic growth. At a minimum, however, planners promised to construct recreation areas in the right-of-way area and include a place for mass transit facilities between roads.

But none of this was feasible politically. In the first place, the proponents of alternative highway building strategies were as divided as supporters of standard forms of road construction. Usually toll road advocates favored decentralized construction and private development; city planners and their colleagues favored national direction of the economy as well as social affairs. Members of the Bragdon group assumed a third point of view. They were centralizers in terms of road building, but perceived their efforts as a contribution to unlimited economic growth. In the meanwhile, downtown business groups, local engineers as well as many many planners rejected these schemes as utopian, hoping to bolster CBD [Central Business District] property values with expressways. In the end, even the promise of $25 billion for the construction of Interstate roads could not abate political conflict between proponents of alternative forms of road building.

Alternative schemes also lacked political support. By definition, they fell outside of the mainstream of American road politics. Since 1921, road engineers, highway users and most members of the incumbent administration had favored road building which served traffic, not schemes for social and economic regeneration. Most Americans looked at road construction in these terms as well. Whenever they had a chance, they voted to limit gasoline tax revenues to road construction, keeping them from the general fund and dispersion to other state services. Members of the Bragdon group, including Secretary of the Treasury Humphrey, tried to break this pattern. While they were divided over a number of matters and inept and obsequious in others, they managed to produce a thoughtful plan for tollway construction. But it was a radical proposal in most respects, destroying established patterns of federal road construction. General Clay was probably correct in his prediction that the implementation of portions of their scheme would produce a " 'revolution' " in some areas of the country.

Deadlock and political conflict were part of the larger American scene. America was a divided nation. While economics was at the heart of many disputes, a narrow definition of social obligations widened the gulf between Americans further. Certainly race was a source of much bitterness. Throughout this century Blacks and Whites have competed for employment, housing and access to political institutions. Ethno-cultural disputes cut through the society as well. Factions of Protestants and Catholics have sought, sometimes with remarkable success, to prescribe forms of worship and pleasure for one-another. Business groups have also been divided. When it seemed appropriate, they turned to government agencies for aid in crushing competitors or blocking unfavorable action by other business groups. All the while, huge bureaucracies emerged to handle the day-to-day problems of a complex social order. In many cases, they turned their attention to gathering greater influence within the affairs of their neighbors. In turn, these efforts were resisted vigorously. During the past decade, the war in Vietnam added another source of tension and conflict between Americans. By the late 1960's, indeed, sheer force constituted one of the primary factors holding American society intact.

One of the key factors in the development of these disputes was the lack of external controls from government and trade associations and no more than formal adherence by their members to unifying norms. There was a consensus of sorts on certain core values such as private property and individualism, and most Americans at least genuflected before the ideals of thrift, diligence and equality of opportunity. But political parties and government agencies as well as business and professional groups reflected a particular view of things. Their perceptions of the nation's needs were rooted in narrow definitions of industrial and professional welfare and the exigencies of bureaucratic survival. As a result, they were restricted in their ability to determine common values. In a fragmented society, there were few who would accept their prescriptions anyway.

Henry Ford II: In Defense of the Automobile

Automobile manufacturers are dependent upon highway construction. By the mid-sixties, with urban expressways now under increasing attack, the automobile manufacturers felt threatened. One of their major arguments was presented by Henry Ford II, Chairman of the Board of Ford Motor Company in a speech to the Young Men's Business Club of New Orleans in July of 1966. It is also significant that he recognized the support of Congressman Hale Boggs, one of the congressional leaders who helped create the Interstate system ten years earlier. Ford's conclusion is important: "As far as urban transportation is concerned, what people want is clear. They have voted overwhelmingly in favor of the automobile" (*Alternative 1*).

Document†

The Highway System
THE NEEDS OF THE CITIES
By HENRY FORD II, *Chairman of the Board, Ford Motor Company*
*Addressed to the Young Men's Business Club of Greater New Orleans,
July 21, 1966*

I am very pleased to join in the recognition being given this evening to our guest of honor. To praise Hale Boggs in New Orleans is obviously superfluous. His countless friends and admirers in this city have been giving him the finest kind of testimonial every other November for the past quarter of a century. His colleagues have confirmed the judgment of his constituents by elevating him to the third highest position in the majority party in the House of Representatives.

His abilities have made Hale Boggs a man of power and influence. But my own admiration for him is based on other qualities as well—his balanced judgment, his humanity, the breadth and depth of his convictions. His rare understanding of the problems and the constructive role of business in our national life makes it especially appropriate that he should be honored by

†From: Henry Ford II, "The Highway System: the Needs of the Cities," *Vital Speeches*, September, 1966, pp. 690-94.

being selected as a life member of the Young Men's Business Club of New Orleans.

Ford Motor Company has been a part of the scene in Louisiana for many years. Some of you younger young businessmen may not know that we had an assembly plant in New Orleans from 1923 to 1932. We now have a parts depot and four other offices here.

This afternoon I had the pleasure of announcing our decision to build a new battery manufacturing plant at one of three sites now being considered in Louisiana. I want to thank Senator Long, Governor McKeithen and many others who have had a hand in bringing Ford manufacturing operations back to Louisiana.

I also want to thank the Board of Administrators of Hale Boggs' alma mater, Tulane University, for making possible another expansion of Ford operations right here in New Orleans. We have recently concluded negotiations with them for a very desirable piece of property at the corner of Canal and Claiborne, on which an outstanding dealership will be built. We will be working with Mr. Louis J. Roussel who will develop this property, only a part of which will be occupied by our dealership.

Our expansion in this part of the country is a direct reflection of the growth of our business here. Since 1950, total motor vehicle registrations in Louisiana have more than doubled, from about 700,000 to nearly 1.5 million.

What has been happening here has been happening all over the country. Car and truck sales in 1964, 1965 and 1966 will total well over 30 million units—an unprecedented sales rate.   When so many people buy our products the automobile industry must be doing something right. You would never know it if you have been listening to our critics. Just when the popularity of our products has been rising most rapidly, people who dislike automobiles as much as most people like them have become more vocal and influential than ever before.

This criticism is partly a reflection of the very real problems caused by rapid growth in the use of motor vehicles. We in the automobile industry do not deny the seriousness of such problems as traffic safety, air pollution and highway congestion. In fact, we emphasize them because we believe we have a responsibility to help solve them—and because we know that the continued growth of our business depends on making the automobile more useful to the American people, and easier for them to live with.

Finding solutions is no easy task, and good answers will not be found if the task is approached in a spirit of retribution which fails to recognize the benefits as well as the problems of increasing highway travel.

The public interest is not served when hostile critics gain such influence that even bad proposals can be adopted as long as they are directed against the automobile and its makers and its users. This, I believe, is what is happening right now. I think the American people should be concerned when this trend threatens to deprive them of what they so clearly want—more and better highway transportation.

Let me give you an example. In many ways, the bill passed by the Senate to regulate the safety characteristicss of automobiles is a good bill. If soundly administered, it can do a great deal to improve traffic safety. But it also contains some features that will not advance safety significantly and could cost the American consumer dearly.

One is the provision that a standard must go into effect within six months to a year after it is announced by the Secretary of Commerce, unless he issues a special exemption. This makes no sense whatever.

In the first place, it will not materially speed up genuine safety advances. Safety improvements can't just be pulled out of thin air. Passing a law won't change the fact that important innovations cannot be designed, tested, proven and tooled in so short a period.

This provision of the bill cannot do much good, but it could do a great deal of harm. The economics and technology of our industry are such that we have to plan product changes two to four years in advance. To cover very high tooling costs, we have to count on a full year's use for all our tooling, and on up to three years for much of it. If the timing of standards does not take these facts into account, it will seriously retard the entire process of product improvement—including safety improvement—add very substantially to the costs of making and owning cars, and reduce our industry's important contributions to the growth of the national economy.

That, at least, is how I see it. Maybe there is a good case on the other side, but I haven't heard it. The significant thing to me is that we haven't even been able to get a good argument going. We've tried hard to make our case, but in today's climate, there is little interest in such practical considerations.

Let me emphasize that we support the general purposes and most of the particulars of the current traffic safety legislation. We are opposed only to some specific provisions that could penalize the car owner and curtail the economic contribution of the auto industry without doing anybody much good.

Safety is only one of the issues that have been seized upon to support such proposals. The automobile is charged, among other things, with strangling cities, spawning suburban sprawl, covering the countryside with pavement, and driving the railroads into bankruptcy.

The critics would have us believe that the automobile is a monster that has run out of control and taken over our lives. The city, they say, has no more room for cars. Let's keep them out, and if people want to come into the city, let them use some form of mass transit—preferably one that runs on rails.

The mounting attack on the automobile has already led to abandonment or long delays in the building of some badly needed expressways. I am pleased to note, however, that your own city expects to complete its portion of the Interstate System well ahead of the 1972 deadline.

Another threat to automobile owners lies in the increasing number of proposals to tax the car user for the benefit of the transit user—thus raising the cost of driving and reducing the already inadequate funds for highways.

Some of our critics seem to feel that the government should plan cities and transportation to reflect their own conception of the ideal city, regardless of what people prefer.

This is nonsense. The market place and the government are different ways of serving the only end a democracy can serve—providing what people want. Sometimes the best way to do this is through business enterprise and free markets. Sometimes, government is the best way. Sometimes people vote with their dollars; sometimes with ballots. But the goal is always the same—providing what people want. As far as urban transportation is concerned, what people want is clear. They have voted overwhelmingly in favor of the automobile.

Passenger car mileage in urban areas nearly tripled between 1940 and 1964. Meanwhile, urban transit patronage has steadily declined from the World War II high, and is now only a little more than half of the 1940 level.

Three-fourths of the transit passengers now ride in buses that use the same highways as the passenger car, and three-fourths of the remaining rail passengers are in the New York City area. Transit is used mainly for commuting in the big cities. But even in the 30 biggest metropolitan areas, only one worker out of four uses public transit to get to work.

This is not to say that there are no problems connected with the rapid growth of automobile travel in urban areas. Changes in public policy to cope with urban traffic congestion are badly needed. Urban transportation planning must be strengthened and in many cities public transit must be improved.

My main point is simply this: to be successful, urban transportation planning must be in harmony with the overwhelming mandate the people have given the automobile. The purpose of metropolitan planning is not to provide what the planners decide people should have—even if they don't want it—but to develop better ways of giving people what they do want and are willing to pay for.

Against this background, I want to take a look at some of the specific issues in urban transportation planning. Perhaps the best place to begin is to consider whether there are any realistic alternatives to the automobile as the predominant mode of urban transportation.

There has been a lot of talk for a long time about people tubes, monorails and other developments that will supposedly make the automobile obsolete. At Ford, we are vitally interested in all new developments in transportation, and in the market potential for all forms of transportation equipment. The fact is, however, that for most travel purposes, no vehicles have yet been developed or are even in prospect that equal the automobile for speed comfort, convenience, privacy, economy and other qualities that people value.

Public transit has one big advantage over car travel. When many people want to travel at the same time along the same route, transit is sometimes cheaper. Door-to-door, it is seldom faster. Transit is at its best for transportation into, out of, and within busy downtown areas. In addition to the preference for auto travel, the basic reason why transit is declining is that most big downtown areas are not as busy as they used to be.

Almost all population growth is now concentrated in the suburbs. Most large cities are losing employment and population and are therefore generating less and less travel, while travel within the suburbs is expanding rapidly. Only 5 to 10 percent of all trips in metropolitan areas begin or end downtown. Because the other 90 to 95 percent of all trips are spread over so large an area, very few suburban routes have enough traffic to justify transit service. What is left for public transit, therefore, is mainly a minor share of the dwindling volume of downtown commuter travel.

This is not to belittle the importance of good transit facilities. In our larger cities, public transit is essential to help meet peak commuter demands. It is also essential to provide adequate mobility within downtown areas and service for those who cannot drive or cannot afford a car.

It is important, however, to recognize that transit can serve only a small fraction of the total transportation demands of urban areas. The new rail transit system being built in San Francisco will handle no more than 5 percent of the total travel needs of the area.

A recent study by the Rand Corporation concluded that rail transit is most likely to make sense in those few cities that already have a substantial investment in rail facilities. Elsewhere, as your own city has decided, equivalent or better service can be provided at much lower cost by buses using the same roads that are also needed for private cars and for the rapidly growing volume of truck transportation.

With all the emphasis now being given to improving rail transit, the opportunities for modernizing bus transit are often neglected.

In short, transit systems are an essential supplement to private cars and highways, but they are not a substitute for cars—and they are even less a substitute for highways. The only real choice our cities face is between less mobility, if highway systems lag behind, or more mobility through better highways and better use of highways.

The growth of the auto-oriented suburbs has created serious problems for the central city, but the city's problems cannot be solved by encouraging transit at the expense of the automobile. Cities that have well developed transit systems are losing jobs and population to the suburbs at least as fast as other cities that rely more heavily on private cars.

Any city that tries to limit its accessibility by automobile will only succeed in cutting itself off from its surrounding territory—and this is hardly the way to solve the city's problems. On the contrary, cities will thrive in the future only to the extent that they strengthen their links with the expanding suburbs.

Those who would curtail the automobile and promote mass transit frequently argue that the automobile has succeeded only because of huge subsidies represented by governmental investment in highways. This, they say, has put mass transit at an unfair disadvantage.

In fact, the shoe is on the other foot. All studies that have been made by the Federal Government show that the highway user pays, through special taxes, much more than his fair share of the costs of roads and streets. Moreover, a large part of the revenue generated by urban traffic is spent on rural roads. Consequently, urban highway users, as a group, are being substantially overcharged.

In terms of costs per mile of roadway, urban expressways are expensive. But since they carry so much traffic so efficiently, they are the cheapest of all roads in terms of costs per mile of travel and they therefore generate the largest excess of revenues over costs. This means that urban expressways users, as a group, are overcharged more than any other drivers. On the other hand, passenger revenues usually do not cover the full cost of transit service, and transit riders therefore are often subsidized by taxpayers. Virtually all rail transit passengers are heavily subsidized.

Nevertheless, we are hearing more and more these days of the argument that car user taxes should be raised in order to pay for improvements in transit systems. The logic is that with higher driving costs and better transit some people would stop driving to the city. This would reduce traffic congestion for the remaining drivers, who should therefore be happy to pay for better transit.

This is like saying that if you like bourbon, you should pay me to drink gin so there will be more bourbon left for you. Even if you can swallow that logic, there is another fallacy in this argument. Experiments in various cities have proved that transit improvement is a very expensive way to get a very small number of cars off the highways in peak travel hours.

There is a very good reason why this is so. In large, congested cities, most commuters already use transit facilities. Traffic studies show that from 60 to 80 percent of all the downtown drivers at peak hours are passing through without stopping. They don't use transit because it can't take them where they want to go. They clog city streets because adequate modern expressway systems by-passing the city have not yet been built.

This brings me to the most important point I want to make this evening. Some of the critics of the automobile charge that it is totally impossible to untangle city traffic by improving highways. They argue that more highways only attract more traffic, until there is no more room for highways—and traffic is just as bad as ever.

This is simply not true. Because of the continuing movement of both jobs and people to the suburbs, present traffic demands are the highest that most cities will be expected to meet, and they are well within limits that can readily be met. Expressways now planned for large urban areas will occupy less than three percent of the land in those areas. The new expressways will carry half of all traffic—thus greatly relieving congestion on other streets.

In spite of all the talk about traffic strangulation, traffic in most cities is flowing more freely than ever before, especially where modern expressway systems are well advanced. In Los Angeles, for instance, average speeds on trips leaving downtown at peak hours have increased by eight miles per hour since 1957.

Although newly opened urban expressways are often crowded to capacity during peak hours, they are now crowded with new traffic, but with cars that formerly used city streets. It may be frustrating to average 30 miles per hour on a new highway designed for 60, but the result is still a large net reduction in travel time.

It is important to remember that much less than half of the urban portion of the Interstate System is now in operation. Traffic is still congested in many cities not because better highways don't work but because we have hardly begun to make up for decades of urban highway neglect.

Like other changes in a dynamic society, urban expressway construction often involves difficult problems such as the need to relocate people and business and to protect aesthetic and historical values. Public acceptance of new urban highways in the future will depend on the extent to which highway planners succeed in solving these problems.

In recent years, imaginative solutions have been developed which prove that new expressways need not disrupt a city's life nor destroy its distinctive features. On the contrary, with proper planning, expressways can make an important contribution to the quality of urban life. They can provide a desirable separation between industrial and residential areas. They can reduce the heavy flow of traffic on local streets. Together with area redevelopment programs, expressways make it possible to devote much less land to streets and to provide much more land for pedestrians, parks and taxable buildings.

Expressways can help to solve, not only the traffic problems, but the broader problems of our major cities.

On the other hand, new highway construction is not the only solution to urban traffic problems. Modern traffic engineering methods and technology have enormous potential. An experimental, computer-operated system to control entry to Chicago's Eisenhower Freeway has increased rush hour capacity, doubled speeds, reduced the period of rush hour congestion by a full hour and cut accidents by 20 percent. Today, no American city has a really modern traffic control system. Except for a few experimental installations, expressways have no traffic control system at all.

At Ford we are investigating a number of different approaches to the application of space-age technology to traffic control and driver information systems. In the not very distant future, we foresee the possible development of a nationwide traffic control system based on earth survey satellites or aerial reconnaissance linked by computer to urban traffic control centers and finally to the stoplight on the corner and even to the radio in your car.

As fantastic as it may seem, we believe such a system will be technically feasible and economically sound. It could make a major contribution to highway efficiency by producing information available in no other way. It could improve highway safety by reducing traffic bottlenecks and providing better knowledge of the causes of accidents. The same aerial survey system could also be useful in solving other problems such as water shortages, air pollution and over-all urban planning.

Experience in designing and operating the manned space flight control center at Houston has given our Philco subsidiary the technical capacity to develop this approach. Our plans are well advanced and we look forward to presenting them to the government soon.

The present highway transportation system is the result of a partnership between government, which provides the highways, and industry, which provides the vehicles. At this point in the evolution of highway transportation, it seems to be both logical and necessary that government and industry join together to develop better and safer ways of managing the use of vehicles on highways. This is how government and industry should work together to serve the interests and the wants of the American people.

The highway system is a vital part of our national life and our national economy. It is now suffering severe growing pains manifested in such problems as traffic safety, air pollution, traffic congestion and the restructuring of our cities. With goodwill, understanding and cooperation between government and industry, these problems can be solved and the American people can continue to enjoy the benefit of increasing mobility.

The problems will not be solved and the benefits will not be available if, as a nation, we give heed to those who would set government and industry against each other, thwart the clear will of the people and turn back to outmoded ways of living and traveling.

7

Lyndon Johnson's Message on Transportation, 1966

Historians may very well point to the leadership of Lyndon B. Johnson as providing the catalyst of developing a more balanced urban transportation system. On March 2, 1966, President Lyndon B. Johnson sent to the Congress his "Message on Transportation," in which he spelled out the deficiencies of federal transportation policy, together with a series of recommendations. In that same year Congress established the Department of Transportation as a means of coordinating the nation's transportation programs (*Alternative 2*). This presidential message meshed neatly with Johnson's efforts to build a "Great Society" in which he attempted for the first time to deal with the qualitative aspects of American life. At the same time his administration was well into its antipoverty efforts, had launched the Model Cities program, and was beginning to develop a new approach to urban housing needs.

Document†

Two centuries ago the American nation came into being. Thirteen sparsely populated colonies, strung out along the Atlantic Seaboard for 1,300 miles, joined their separate wills in a common endeavor.

Three bonds united them.

There was the cultural bond of a single language.

There was the moral bond of a thirst for liberty and democratic government.

There was the physical bond of a few roads and rivers, by which the citizens of the colonies engaged in peaceful commerce.

Two centuries later the language is the same. The thirst for liberty and democracy endures.

The physical bond—that tenuous skein of rough trails and primitive roads—has become a powerful network on which the prosperity and convenience of our society depend.

In a nation that spans a continent, transportation is the web of union.

†From: Lyndon B. Johnson, "Message on Transportation," *Presidential Papers of Lyndon B. Johnson, 1966* (Washington, D.C.: Government Printing Office, 1967), vol. 1, pp. 250-63.

THE GROWTH OF OUR TRANSPORTATION SYSTEM. It is not necessary to look back to the 1760s to chronicle the astonishing growth of American transportation. Twenty years ago there were 31 million motor vehicles in the United States. Today there are 90 million. By 1975 there will be nearly 120 million.

Twenty years ago there were 1.5 million miles of paved roads and streets in the United States. Today this figure has almost doubled.

Twenty years ago there were 38,000 private and commercial aircraft. Today there are more than 97,000.

Twenty years ago commercial airlines flew 209 million miles. Last year [1965] they flew one billion miles.

Twenty-five years ago American transportation moved 619 billion ton-miles of cargo. In 1964, 1.5 trillion ton-miles were moved.

The manufacturing of transportation equipment has kept pace. It has tripled since 1947. Last year $4.5 billion was spent for new transportation plant and equipment.

Transportation is one of America's largest employers. There are:

737,000 railroad employees

270,000 local and interurban workers

230,000 in air transport

Almost a million men and women in motor transport and storage

Together with pipeline and water transportation employees, the total number of men and women who earn their livelihoods by moving people and goods is well over 2.5 million.

The Federal Government supports or regulates almost every means of transportation. Last year alone more than $5 billion in Federal funds were invested in transportation—in highway construction, in river and harbor development, in airway operation and airport construction, in maritime subsidies. The Government owns 1,500 of the nation's 2,500 oceangoing cargo vessels.

Our transportation system—the descendant of the horse-drawn coaches and sailing ships of Colonial times—accounts for one in every six dollars in the American economy. In 1965, that amounted to $120 billion—a sum greater than the gross national product of this nation in 1940.

SHORTCOMINGS OF OUR SYSTEM. Vital as it is, mammoth and complex as it has become, the American transportation system is not good enough.

It is not good enough when it offers nearly a mile of street or road for every square mile of land—and yet provides no relief from time-consuming, frustrating and wasteful congestion.

It is not good enough when it produces sleek and efficient jet aircraft—and yet cannot move passengers to and from airports in the time it takes those aircraft to fly hundreds of miles.

It is not good enough when it builds superhighways for supercharged automobiles—and yet cannot find a way to prevent 50,000 highway deaths this year.

It is not good enough when public and private investors pour $15 million into a large, high-speed ship—only to watch it remain idle in port for days before it is loaded.

It is not good enough when it lays out new freeways to serve new cities and suburbs—and carelessly scars the irreplaceable countryside.

It is not good enough when it adheres to custom for its own sake—and ignores opportunities to serve our people more economically and efficiently.

It is not good enough if it responds to the needs of an earlier America—and does not help us expand our trade and distribute the fruits of our land throughout the world.

WHY WE HAVE FALLEN SHORT. Our transportation system has not emerged from a single drawing board, on which the needs and capacities of our economy were all charted. It could not have done so, for it grew along with the country itself—now restlessly expanding, now consolidating, as opportunity grew bright or dim. Thus, investment and service innovations responded to special needs. Research and development were sporadic, sometimes inconsistent, and largely oriented toward the promotion of a particular means of transportation.

As a result, America today lacks a coordinated transportation system that permits travelers and goods to move conveniently and efficiently from one means of transportation to another, using the best characteristics of each.

Both people and goods are compelled to conform to the system as it is, despite the inconvenience and expense of:

Aging and often obsolete transportation plant and equipment

Networks chiefly designed to serve a rural society

Services long outstripped by our growing economy and population, by changes in land use, by new concepts in industrial plant location, warehousing and distribution

The failure to take full advantage of new technologies developed elsewhere in the economy

Programs and policies which impede private initiative and dull incentives for innovation

The result is waste—of human and economic resources—and of the taxpayer's dollar. . . .

If the growth of our transport industries merely keeps pace with our current national economic growth, the demand for transportation will more than double in the next twenty years.

But even that is too conservative an estimate. Passenger transportation is growing much faster than our gross national product—reflecting the desires of an affluent people with ever increasing incomes.

PRIVATE AND PUBLIC RESPONSIBILITY. The United States is the only major nation in the world that relies primarily upon privately owned and operated transportation. . . .

But private ownership has been made feasible only by the use of publicly granted authority and the investment of public resources—

By the construction of locks, dams, and channels on our rivers and inland waterways

By the development of a vast highway network

By the construction and operation of airports and airways

by the development of ports and harbors

By direct financial support of the merchant marine

By grants of eminent domain authority

By capital equipment grants and demonstration projects for mass transit

In years past, by grants of public land to assist the railroads

Enlightened government has served as a full partner with private enterprise in meeting America's urgent need for mobility.

That partnership must now be strengthened with all the means that creative federalism can provide. The costs of a transportation paralysis in the years ahead are too severe. The rewards of an efficient system are too great. We cannot afford the luxury of drift—or proceed with "business as usual." . . .

A DEPARTMENT OF TRANSPORTATION. I urge the Congress to establish a Cabinet-level department of transportation. . . .

The department of transportation will:

Coordinate the principal existing programs that promote transportation in America

Bring new technology to a total transportation system, by promoting research and development in cooperation with private industry

Improve safety in every means of transportation

Encourage private enterprise to take full and prompt advantage of new technology opportunities

Encourage high-quality, low cost service to the public

Conduct systems analyses and planning, to strengthen the weakest parts of today's systems

Develop investment criteria and standards, and analytical techniques to assist all levels of government and industry in their transportation investments.

SAFETY. 105,000 Americans died in accidents last year [1965].

More than half were killed in transportation, or in recreation accidents related to transportation.

49,000 deaths involved motor vehicles.

1,300 involved aircraft.

1,500 involved ships and boats.

2,300 involved railroads.

Millions of Americans were injured in transportation accidents—the overwhelming majority involving automobiles.

Each means of transportation has developed safety programs of varying effectiveness. Yet we lack a comprehensive program keyed to a total transportation system.

Proven safety techniques in one means have not always been adapted in others.

Last year the highway death toll set a new record. The prediction for this year is that more than 50,000 persons will die on our streets and highways—more than 50,000 useful and promising lives will be lost, and as many families stung by grief.

The toll of Americans killed in this way since the introduction of the automobile is truly unbelievable. It is 1.5 million—more than all the combat deaths suffered in all our wars.

No other necessity of modern life has brought more convenience to the American people—or more tragedy—than the automobile. . . .

RESEARCH AND DEVELOPMENT. Today, the United States ranks as the world's leader in technology.

Despite this—and despite the importance of transportation in the competition for international trade—exclusive of national security and space, the Federal Government spends less than 1 percent of its total research and development budget for transportation.

Under our system of Government, private enterprise bears the primary responsibility for research and development in the transportation field.

But the Government can help. It can plan and fashion research and development for a total transportation system which is beyond the responsibility or capability of private industry.

Through Government-sponsored research and development we can:

Fully understand the complex relationships among the components of a total transportation system

Provide comprehensive and reliable data for both private and public decisions

Identify areas of transportation which can be exploited by private industry to provide safer and more efficient services to the public

Build the basis for a more efficient use of public resources

Provide the technological base needed to assure adequate domestic and international transportation in times of emergency

Help make significant advances in every phase of transport—in aircraft, in oceangoing ships, in swifter rail service, in safer vehicles

The department of transportation—working with private industry and other Government agencies—will provide a coordinated program of research and development to move the nation toward our transportation goals. The department can help translate scientific discovery into industrial practice. . . .

ADVANCED LAND TRANSPORT [In 1965] . . . Congress took a long step towards advanced land transportation by enacting the high-speed ground transportation research and development program. This program will be continued at the most rapid pace consistent with sound management of the research effort.

Similar vision and imagination can be applied to highway transport.

Segments of the interstate highway network already in operation are the most efficient, productive roads ever built anywhere in the world. Motor vehicles move at higher rates of speed, more safely and in greater number per lane than on conventional roads. Transportation costs are reduced, and less land area is needed for this volume of traffic.

With the network about half completed after ten years, it is apparent that interstate highways, as well as other roads and streets, can become ever more productive and safe.

Accordingly, I am directing the Secretary of Commerce to:

Investigate means for providing guidance and control mechanisms to increase the capacity and improve the safety of our highway network

Conduct research into the means of improving traffic flow—particularly in our cities—so we can make better use of our existing roads and streets

Investigate potential of separate roadways for various classes of vehicles, with emphasis on improving mass transportation service.

SYSTEMS RESEARCH. Some of our brightest opportunities in research and development lie in the less obvious and often neglected parts of our transportation system.

We spend billions for constructing new highways, but comparatively little for traffic control devices.

We spend millions for fast jet aircraft but little on the traveler's problem of getting to and from the airport.

We have mounted a sizable Government-industry program to expand exports, yet we allow a mountain of red-tape paperwork to negate our efforts. Worldwide, a total of 810 forms are required to cover all types of cargo imported and exported. In this country alone, as many as forty-three separate forms are used in one export shipment. Eighty separate forms may be needed to process some imports. This is paperwork run wild.

I am directing the Secretaries of Treasury and Commerce and the Attorney General to attack these problems through the use of effective systems research programs. And I have directed them to eliminate immediately every unnecessary element of red tape that inhibits our import and export programs.

TRANSPORTATION FOR AMERICA. The Founding Fathers rode by stage to Philadelphia to take part in the Constitutional Convention. They could not have anticipated the immense complexity—or the problems—of transportation in our day.

Yet they, too, recognized the vital national interest in commerce between the states. The early Congresses expressed that interest even more directly, by supporting the development of road and waterway systems.

Most important, the Founding Fathers gave us a flexible system of government. Cities, states and the Federal Government can join together—and in many cases work with private enterprise—in partnerships of creative federalism to solve our most complex problems.

For the very size of our transportation requirements—rising step-by-step with the growth of our population and industry—demands that we respond with new institutions, new programs of research, new efforts to make our vehicles safe, as well as swift.

Modern transportation can be the rapid conduit of economic growth—or a bottleneck.

It can bring jobs and loved ones and recreation closer to every family—or it can bring instead sudden and purposeless death.

It can improve every man's standard of living—or multiply the cost of all he buys.

It can be a convenience, a pleasure, the passport to new horizon of the mind and spirit—or it can frustrate and impede and delay.

The choice is ours to make.

We build the cars, the trains, the planes, the ships, the roads and the airports. We can, if we will, plan their safe and efficient use in the decades ahead to improve the quality of life for all Americans.

The program I have outlined in this message is the first step toward that goal.

I urge its prompt enactment by the Congress.

8

"The Future of the Automobile"

By 1969 the American automobile industry had begun to sense definite changes in American taste and preferences in automobiles. The seemingly endless problems of air pollution, traffic safety, growing small car foreign competition, urban freeway routing, traffic congestion, and spiralling costs were definitely having an impact upon millions of Americans. Many of these changes are captured in an illuminating interview conducted by *U.S. News and World Report* with the Chairman of the board of General Motors, James M. Roche.

Document†

Q Mr. Roche, is there any real measure of the role the automobile industry plays in America's economy?

A I think it is perhaps the most important single factor. The automobile industry and related industries involved in maintaining our motorized-transportation system account for one out of every six jobs in this country.

To look beyond the economic impact, we enjoy the highest degree of personal mobility ever achieved by any people in the world. This has been a very important factor in enabling us to accomplish what we have.

Roughly 80 per cent of American families own at least one car. There are 88 million motor vehicles registered in the United States—73 million passenger cars and about 15 million trucks—the backbone of our transportation system.

Another measuring stick is the vast quantity of basic materials we use: 61 per cent of the rubber consumed in the U.S., a third of all the glass, 20 per cent of the steel and 10 per cent of the aluminum—just to mention a few items.

Q Would you characterize autos as a growth industry?

A Yes, very definitely.

In calendar year 1968 there were 9.6 million passenger cars sold in the United States. The normal trend line for 1968 calendar year indicated a volume of 9 million. We were 600,000 above.

We think that by 1975 normal volume can very well get up to, say, 11.5 million, and by 1980 it will probably get in the area of 13.5 million. This includes both imported and domestic cars.

†From: *U.S. News and World Report,* February 10, 1969, pp. 64-71. Copyright 1969 U.S. News & World Report, Inc.

The imports, of course, were a rather important factor last year—about 10.2 per cent of 1968 sales.

Q How much of the current demand is for replacements?

A Last year about 6.8 million cars were scrapped. Eight or 10 years ago that number alone would have been regarded as a very satisfactory year in new-car production.

Q What about growth in car ownership?

A Growth in registrations last year was around 2.6 million to 2.8 million.

Q Were many of those cars bought by two-car families?

A Yes. I would guess that more than 25 percent of all families have two or more cars, and the proportion is growing all the time.

Q What will the automobile population be by 1980?

A Somewhere in the area of 115 million automobiles and trucks.

Q Is the time coming when the country will have all the cars it wants or can use?

A We don't think so. There was a saturation point forecast a long time ago—I think in 1927—when we had 21.5 million vehicles. A very prominent economist in the Middle West said that this was as far as the automobile industry was going to go; that the saturation point had been reached; that the purchasing power of the people, combined with the road system, made it impossible for the automobile industry to progress beyond that point.

Q But isn't there a limit to the number of cars, in terms of roads and parking, in places such as New York City?

A Obviously, we have to find a way to take care of the growing number of cars. We're going to have to find parking facilities, build roads, throughways, freeways—whatever you want to call them—to accommodate this growth. Up to now, we have been fairly successful in doing that.

Q Would it help to make cars smaller?

A Well, cars are smaller. Prior to, say, the 1960 model year, pretty much all domestic cars would have been categorized as "regular size." Since then the percentage of regular-size cars has declined, so that today it's roughly 55 percent of the total. This means that the small and intermediate cars are accounting for about 45 percent of the domestic output. On top of that, most of the imported cars can be catalogued as small cars.

Q Haven't sales of imported cars been increasing faster than those of domestic cars?

A Yes.

Q Does this mean the foreign manufacturers have caught on to something you haven't caught on to?

A I don't think that it does. I think the increase in the sale of imported cars is a further indication of the great variety of uses and needs for transportation in the United States. The imported cars—the growth of them, of course, is pretty much in the postwar period, not only here but in the countries where they're produced, and we operate in some of those countries.

There the transition in the postwar period was from a bicycle to a motorcycle to a small car. And the small car, in essence, was just basic transportation. It had to be low-cost, and performance was not too much of a factor. Fuel economy and economy of operation were very important factors. The purchasers of these cars were willing to sacrifice comfort, appearance in some cases, and performance in order to achieve other objectives.

In this country, in many instances, imports have been used as a second or third car for shopping, or for the kids to go to school, or for the wife to use when the husband is working. The need for this kind of car is certainly very evident in our economy.

We know how to build small cars. We do build small cars. We're going to build a new one—smaller than any we're building today. We're currently under way with this car. It will not be on the market until mid-1970. We think it will be very competitive with the foreign imports.

This car is going to be about a foot shorter in over-all length than any car we make today. It will be about 11 inches longer than the most popular import, which is the Volkswagen. It will weigh roughly 1,900 pounds, maybe a little bit more—600 to 700 pounds lighter in weight than the small Chevy II, for example. It will have passenger space, trunk space far superior to the small imports today. And it will have performance—acceleration ability, for example—that is superior to these cars. And it will have fuel economy that's comparable.

Q How can you afford to build a car in the price range of an import with the difference in wage rates paid in Europe and here?

A That's a good question. We're very much concerned about that, and that is the reason why we have not gone into this before—not because we didn't know how to make a small car.

We make the Opel Kadett in Germany, which is very competitive with Volkswagen in markets around the world and becoming more competitive in the United States. We sold 85,000 Kadetts in the United States last year.

Q Why not produce the Kadett over here?

A We could, but to produce the Kadett in the United States would cost enough more so that we couldn't market it economically.

Q What reason is there to think you will do better with a new small car?

A Because it is going to be differently designed. It's going to have some new manufacturing techniques and procedures that we have not used in other cars. We are hopeful that, with this approach, we're going to be able to produce this car competitively.

Q Will it be priced at about $2,000?

A That's the price range of the Kadett and the Volkswagen today, and we expect to be competitive with that.

Q In some respects the manufacturing of this car is going to be revolutionary—

A Yes.

Q Do you think it will lead the way to savings in the cost of making other types of automobiles?

A Possibly. We don't know this yet, but this will be a more simple car to produce than any of the present domestic models.

Q Will you sell it abroad?

A We expect to export it wherever we export other cars. We sell a few cars in almost every country, but we run into terrific problems—not only tariffs but discriminatory taxes which are levied against horsepower and weight.

Q Are you doing anything about that?

A We're protesting as loudly as we can, but I wouldn't say the results are very much.

Q Did the United Auto Workers make any concessions in connection with your new small car—such as agreeing to accept a cut in wages?

A No. However, the UAW does not block automation and improved technology. We do have occasional flareups in some plants where, maybe for local-union political reasons, the employees don't take the same approach. But Walter Reuther [president of the UAW] does not oppose technological advances. He recognizes that the success of his union, the progress of his people lie in having a successful company, and if restrictive practices limit the size of that success, he is willing to accept improvements. That's his basic approach.

The UAW, of course, is concerned always about the amount of effort that anybody puts into his work, so the increase in productivity that we're talking about does not result from anybody doing more work—just from the improved methods and better technology.

Q The Government seems to think the drop in our exports of autos, steel, and a couple of other products is responsible for much of our dollar problem. Will your new car help to develop a greater export surplus?

A This car will make a further contribution to it. However, I have seen some of those comments about the balance of payments and I don't agree, because General Motors in 1967—I don't have all the figures in yet for 1968—contributed a favorable balance of payments of about 782 million dollars, and in the whole period since 1946, about 11.5 billion dollars.

Now, that is the excess of our exports over our imports, plus dividend remittances from our operations abroad—something we can't overlook. We think we've been doing a pretty good job. And I'm sure that Ford and Chrysler have figures that are comparable in proportion to their size.

Q Won't your new small car cut into sales of Chevy II's and some other GM autos?

A That's a very good possibility. But we have 160 different GM models today, and every time we decide we're going to bring out a new model or eliminate a model, we have to make a decision with respect to what we think the impact is going to be on some existing line. In this respect our approach to a smaller car is no different.

But in the main, we're looking at this 10 percent of the market—the market for imports—which is not being satisfied by us or anybody else with a domestic product. This is a gamble we have to take, as we see it.

Q Most buyers in this country are looking for something more than just transportation, aren't they?

A Yes. And this has been the experience abroad as well. The foreign cars started out on a very modest basis, but they have been improved—improved braking systems, improved steering systems, radios. Now they are starting to add air conditioning and automatic transmissions.

We just built a new automatic-transmission plant in Strasbourg, France, to serve our German subsidiary, Opel, and our English subsidiary, Vauxhall. Possibly we will sell some of these transmissions to other manufacturers in Europe. The plant represents a very substantial investment on our part and is indicative, I think, of the trend.

Q Can you really challenge Volkswagen in the U.S.? Opel hasn't done it—

A We haven't finished with Opel as yet.

Q Weren't you hoping to sell 100,000 Opels a year in this country?

A We sold 85,000 in '68. Had it not been for some shipping difficulties and a slight delay in the introduction of the current model, the Kadett, we might have made it.

Opel does quite well against the Volkswagen in Germany. There are reasons for that—the distribution system, for one.

We had to start here with the Buick distribution system. So wherever Opel is sold in the United States, it's sold as a dual line with a very popular American line. An Opel Kadett perhaps doesn't get the same intensive sales effort that it would get if it had an exclusive distribution system, as in Germany, where practically every Opel dealer is an exclusive Opel dealer, and that's all he worries about.

Q Who will sell your new small car?

A Chevrolet dealers. Chevrolet has several different lines of cars now and is sort of geared to this type of merchandising.

Q But won't Volkswagen still have something of an advantage on this point of distribution?

A They have a very definite advantage from the distribution standpoint, in my opinion. They've got a well-established dealer organization that's been a successful dealer organization, and they've done a fine job in merchandising the Volkswagen.

Q Will the public know your new car as a Chevrolet?

A Yes. The current name for it is the XP-887, and if you've got a good name, we're in the market.

Q It has to start with a "C," doesn't it?

A Not necessarily. That has been a belief for some time—a common belief, and perhaps not too far wrong. But we've got to come up with a good name for this one. We're working at it.

Rivalry in Auto Industry

Q Mr. Roche, the Federal Government seems at times to feel that General Motors is a near monopoly. Just how much competition is there in the auto industry?

A I've been in the automobile industry for a long time, and I think it is about as competitive as any industry.

General Motors was 60 years old last September 16, and we had a very inauspicious beginning—some very rough years for the first seven or eight years of our existence. As a matter of fact, we almost went bankrupt in 1920 and 1921. We acquired our last passenger-car unit in 1918. That was Chevrolet.

So we have taken what existed on a very precarious level and over this 50-year period we think we have earned—through the products we have been able to build, the satisfaction we've been able to afford the users of these products—the position that we enjoy in the industry.

We live in a very precarious industry.

Q Haven't many auto companies died off?

A They sure have. The public is very fickle.

Back in the days when General Motors was just getting started—in the late teens and the early '20s—Ford had 60 percent of the business, and General Motors had 9, 10, 11 percent. In 1955, our Buick line had about 10 percent of the business. We saw that go down between 1955 and 1959 to about 4 percent.

Q Was that when Government officials were talking about breaking Buick away from General Motors?

A They suggested that when Buick got up to 10 percent of the business. The talk stopped within a couple of years. Buick had a product line that did not satisfy the customers—which is very plain and very simple.

You may remember the more recent experience of Chrysler, which in 1962 got down to around 10 percent of the business. Last year Chrysler got nearly 18 percent.

I think that you don't have to do much more than read the advertisements at the manufacturers' level, at the retail level, take note of the radio and television commercials, or walk into a few dealers' showrooms to find out how competitive the business really is. It is very competitive at the manufacturers' level, and it's very competitive at the dealer level—not only between dealers selling competitive makes of cars but also between dealers selling the same make of car, because in a community like Washington we've probably got half a dozen Chevrolet dealers within a 10 or 15-minute drive from here.

Anybody who says that there isn't competition in the automobile business just doesn't understand. . . .

Aim: Trouble-Free Cars

Q What can you do to make cars more trouble-free?

A We are continually working on this, and have since the beginning of the industry. Think back 15, 20 years ago: We used to recommend that a car be brought in to the dealer every month for inspection and check-over to be sure that everything was in operating condition. We used to recommend an oil change and lubrication every 1,000 miles or every month. Today our oil changes go 4,000 to 6,000 miles. Some points are required to be lubricated only once every 12,000 miles, and some that used to have to be lubricated on schedule are now lubricated for life.

We've made great strides in the durability of the engines. Valve grinding and reboring engines used to be a regular thing. You almost never hear of it any more. The average dealer probably couldn't rebore an engine today.

So these are the areas of progress that we have made.

I had occasion to review the experience of one of our large fleets. Over the last six years there was a reduction of 38 percent in the frequency of service operations required for a car.

Q Were those cars with complicated options on them?

A They had power steering, power brakes and automatic transmissions. Automatic transmissions today are pretty foolproof. These were cars that were used in business fleets.

Q Is there any new development ahead along the same line—to eliminate service problems?

A We are doing a lot of work in the electrical field. This has been the bane of our existence. I don't know if you have ever seen the inside of a door panel—the wiring harnesses that go through a car. This is a very complicated affair—much more complicated than the wiring of a home, where you run a wire from one point to another. We're making some progress in that—toward integrated circuitry, printed circuits, that we think have promise. We're doing a lot of work in areas such as this that we think will pay off.

Q What's the average life of an automobile these days?

A That is difficult to calculate. We know that there are a lot of cars that last up to 25 years. You have some attrition from accidents and abuse. But I would say that, on the basis of just pure statistical numbers, the average life today is about 10 years.

Q What is the most economical point for turning in a car—three years, two years?

A That depends on the individual's requirements—how much and how often he uses the car—and the alternatives. If you drive 25,000 or 30,000 miles a year and have to buy tires and have a maintenance job done on your car, that enters into it.

Q What are people mainly interested in?

A I think they want a combination of things. Appearance is very important. That's the first impression the customers get. But you can't sell a good-looking car that isn't good mechanically and keep it sold for very long.

Q What is happening in the drive to reduce air pollution from auto exhaust?

A We feel we've made very substantial progress. We have a crankcase-ventilating valve, which is the most important breakthrough. That came in California in 1961 and became standard across the country in 1963. That eliminated about 25 percent of the unburned hydrocarbons that were being emitted by an automobile.

Q What about the Justice Department's complaint that GM and others in the industry conspired to delay the use of this system?

A This complaint is entirely unwarranted, in our opinion. More than 15 years ago General Motors and others in the industry launched a program of co-operative research and development to find solutions for the motor-vehicle air-pollution problem. This was done to meet a pressing public need. Public officials had urged the industry to take such a step.

General Motors made major contributions to the joint industry effort, including the discovery of the crankcase as a significant source of emissions. This led to the first significant advance in emission control. We designed valves to control crankcase emissions. The right to use these valves was made freely available to all participants in the industry program.

In turn, General Motors and the public have benefited from discoveries and information furnished by other companies under the program.

It is a great disappointment to have the Government bring these charges regarding a program of 15 years' standing which was entered into in good faith by the companies which have been responsible for most of the progress toward automotive air-pollution control. However, we in General Motors intend to continue to pursue this work as energetically as before.

Q Have there been other developments?

A Yes. We have what we call an air-reactor injector system—an air pump that provides the air to facilitate better combustion. We have another system which we call the controlled-combustion system. We use one of these systems on every car, depending on the type of engine and transmission.

On a 1969 model, the emissions of both unburned hydrocarbons and carbon monoxide have been reduced by about 63 percent, as compared with a car not equipped with these new devices.

Q Those devices require maintenance, don't they?

A Yes, and this is an important factor, because while the system will work when the car is new and perhaps for the first year, it does require maintenance like anything mechanical. Unless the customer does maintain it, the system is not going to be fully effective.

In most cases the dealer would suggest this, but if the customer can't detect any difference in performance of his car—and he can't, in most cases—he may not follow the dealer's advice.

Q Should a check on the air-pollution controls on a car be part of the State automobile inspections?

A I think that's going to come. But at the present state of the art, it requires sophisticated equipment to make the tests. We're working hard to develop a simpler system, but right now we have to use computers, exhaust chambers and dynamometers—it's a real chore to get a reading.

A Look Ahead

Q Will the electric car solve our pollution problem, sofar as the automobile is involved?

A We don't foresee an electric car any time soon. We have electric cars running, but until somebody finds a way to store electrical energy efficiently and in a manner that will permit operation with the range and speed and economy of the cars we are used to today, the electric car is not a likely prospect.

Q Are you working on new types of batteries?

A Yes.

Q Any progress there?

A No. We are unable to see any progress.

Q How about a car that would run on a fuel cell?

A We have a van running with a fuel cell, but I wouldn't want to be close to it if it is ever involved in a collision.

Q Why not?

A Radiation. And there's another minor problem with it. The fuel cell takes up all the cargo space in the van.

Q Are there other types of engines that may take the place of the internal-combustion engine?

A We're working with turbines. We're working with steam engines. We're working with electric motors. We're working with a hybrid engine—an electric system with a little gasoline motor to operate the car and recharge the battery when you get out in an area where pollution may not be as much of a problem. That hybrid engine is a very expensive answer to the problem.

Q Why not go back to a steam engine?

A If we could make the steamer work, that would be good. Insofar as we can see, there is nothing in the foreseeable future that is going to be competitive with internal combustion.

  · Q How about the diesel engine for passenger cars?

A Mercedes-Benz uses that for some cars—taxicabs. I rode from Frankfurt, Germany, to our plant in Wiesbaden one day on the autobahn in a Mercedes diesel taxicab, and I was never so frightened in all my life. The cab used absolutely no acceleration. The driver would start to go around a truck or other vehicle a little slower than ours, and he would get a "beep-beep" from the car behind and would have to get back in line under cover again. He could pass hardly anything.

But the diesel cars are very economical, they're very long-lived, and for taxi service in the city, they probably have a point.

Q How about safety? Is there real progress on that?

A Yes. We're building probably the safest cars we've ever produced.

The federal safety program is a constructive one. Measuring the effect statistically is a very difficult problem because there is a great dearth of statistics with respect to accidents. I think that the attention that's been focused on safety and some of the safety regulations will make a contribution, the full effect of which is not apparent at the present time.

The industry has always been trying to improve the safety of its cars. Certainly we want our customers to live.

We have introduced four-wheel brakes, safety glass, automatic transmissions, more-powerful engines, better bodies, more-rugged frames, power brakes—all things that have improved the safety of our cars. But we cannot control the driver.

We had seat belts available as options on our cars for at least 12 years. When they were optional equipment, people ordered them on only a very small percentage—5 or 6 percent—of the cars that were sold. Today they are on 100 percent of the cars.

There is no question that a seat belt is a very important factor in the case of an accident, and people would be well advised to wear seat belts. This is just incontrovertible. Yet a lot of people don't use them.

I saw a survey the other day which indicated some improvement—that 42 percent of the people now are using seat belts, at least on longer trips. Well, that's not good enough, because exhaustive studies in Michigan of accidents over holidays—Fourth of July, Memorial Day and so on—have found that 80 percent of the fatalities occurred within 25 miles of the victim's home. So the attitude of the motorist has an important bearing on safety.

Shoulder harnesses are another example. They are a little awkward to wear. Maybe someday we'll be smart enough to make them more convenient to wear and easier to adjust. But they, too, make a contribution.

Q Still, doesn't the number of traffic deaths set a new record every year?

A Well, the number of cars is increasing. Deaths per 100 million miles of travel are going down a little bit—not very much, but going down.

On this matter of controlling the driver—a report to Congress last August said that 25,000 of the deaths in the previous year could be attributed in some way to people who were using alcohol. The death toll is about 53,000—so you've got alcohol involved in almost half of them. And the report said 800,000 other accidents involved the use of alcohol. So this is a tremendous part of the accident problem.

Now, the safety program has to be a balanced one. And up to now, most of the attention has been focused on the industry—and logically so perhaps, because we want the vehicles to be as safe as they can possibly be. That's our responsibility—to design them and build them to the best of our ability.

But there are these other factors—driver training, driver licensing laws, traffic control, enforcement of traffic rules, highway construction and design, and compulsory inspection to insure proper maintenance. All of these things have to play a part. . . .

Copyright 1969 U.S. News & World Report, Inc.

9

"Highway in the Urban Scene"

During the late sixties, several books and innumerable articles vigorously attacked the Interstate system. Many lamented the environmental destruction on the countryside, but most tended to focus upon the urban aspect. Perhaps the most widely read and quoted was Helen Leavitt's *Superhighway— Superhoax* (1970). Her caustic, slashing attack reflects well the crusading spirit of antifreeway spokesmen. Couched primarily in moral and environmental, rather than economic terms, Ms. Leavitt declares total war upon the Highway Lobby and its freeways *(Alternative 2).*

Document†

The red, white, and blue shield, patriotic emblem of the National System of Interstate and Defense Highways, is a familiar highway guidepost to American motorists. It is now posted along more than 30,000 miles of superhighways on a network that has been taking shape across the continental United States for more than a decade.

The Interstate Highway System is the largest single public works project ever undertaken by man. As originally projected in 1944, it was to contain 40,000 miles of highways. As approved by a law enacted in 1956, its mileage was boosted to 41,000 miles and its cost was estimated at $27 billion. The system was to be financed by federal and state funds on a 90-10 ratio—Uncle Sam would contribute nearly $25 billion, the states $2.7 billion. The highway network would cross and, in effect, link every state and pass near all major metropolitan areas. It was to be completed by June 1971.

Today, interstate highways extend across open country and mountains, traverse rivers, follow our coastlines, and not only pass near our cities, but actually enter them. Two thirds of the Interstate System has been completed at a cost of $40 billion, a figure already $13 billion greater than the original estimate. The ultimate cost has been estimated at three times the original figure, total mileage has been increased again to 42,500 miles, and the last links are likely to be completed no sooner than 1975—if ever.

Those sections of the system already completed in and around our urban areas are the most heavily used, particularly for suburban commuter trips, rather than for interstate travel. Critics who have questioned the wisdom of

†From: "Highway in the Urban Scene," from *Superhighway—Superhoax* by Helen Leavitt. Copyright ©1970 by Helen Leavitt. Reprinted by permission of Doubleday & Company, Inc., pp. 1-19.

extending sections of the superhighway system into the cores of our cities, which fill up with commuter-trip automobiles, have been told by highway officials and highway boosters that these urban sections of interstate highways are essential to the economy, national defense, and safety of our transportation system. Persistent critics, those who question these premises, are dismissed by officials as fanatics, unpatriotic (since the highway boosters claim the highways serve national defense), or simply uninformed. Those who argue that the cities are being engulfed with commuter automobiles are told this is all the more proof that even more such highways are needed to alleviate congestion.

This urban congestion was not the result of the original nationwide network of highways contemplated in 1944, however. That plan called for bypassing cities in an effort to provide long-haul travel between cities and states. It was not planned for the local commuter traffic we see today. By the time the plan was implemented in 1956, however, there were some beltways and arterials, forerunners of the Interstate System, already built around the perimeters of some of our cities, which in turn encouraged suburban development. The lure of 90 percent federal funding provided the short step which led politicians and highway officials to the conclusion that highways should actually enter our cities. Shortly thereafter, automobile congestion and urban "sprawl" began in earnest, nurtured by our federal highway program.

The superhighways held great promise for the future when the project was still on the drawing board. An article in the December 1956 issue of *Automotive Industries* commented:

> In laying out the general pattern of the 41,000 mile chain of national express routes the planners have steered away from the heavily built-up industrial and residential cores of the cities. Belt lines and bypasses are to allow through traffic on the new system to remain free of urban bottlenecks. Those drivers with destinations downtown will be able to reach them via access thoroughfares, but there is to be no dumping of Interstate traffic in front of city hall.

Another article in the same issue predicted that

> . . . the pressure toward more and more decentralization will become irresistible. The downtown commercial and industrial sites will become things of the past . . . in their place neighborhood units will spring up—pleasant residential areas, made up mostly of medium-sized apartment buildings located close to modern factories and office buildings, thus eliminating the need for a great deal of commuting. . . . Transportation no longer will be a problem. Most people will be able to walk to work. Pedestrian and vehicle traffic ways will be separated, perhaps on different levels, and walking will once more be safe and pleasant. . . . The city would become a pleasant place to work in and to live in; instead of asphalt jungles, the verdant city without suburbs; instead of obsolete street patterns, an efficient, well integrated network of expressways and arterials. In such an environment, the automobile would vastly increase its mobility and therefore become a more valuable part of urban living.

It didn't work out this way in the cities, where 5000 miles of the

Interstate System have already been opened and where 2500 more miles are scheduled to open by 1974. Our great urban centers have been subjected to the busy concrete mixers and asphalt rollers in the guise of progress, where the ribbons of highway they create are further strangling automobile traffic, adding to the already dangerous air pollution levels and displacing the city's residents with still more cars while transportation daily becomes more difficult.

According to the Bureau of Public Roads, federal overseer for the project, the Interstate shield represents the best engineering and design, maximum safety standards, and, ultimately, a transportation system vital to our country's economy and defense. American motorists, says the Bureau, can expect to wheel onto any portion of this gigantic highway system, confident in the knowledge that it represents technological, economical, and social progress. Each completed link adds to the system's emerging form and hastens fulfillment of the highway engineer's ultimate dream—to be able to drive from one corner of the country at high speed to another without stopping for a traffic light.

This view of our highway program is supported by a vast lobby consisting of state highway officials, contractors, auto manufacturers, engineers, congressmen, state legislators, newspaper publishers, and representatives of road users groups. They all know better.

Instead of fulfilling the Bureau's claims, the Interstate System has in effect forced our society to scuttle all forms of transportation except the automobile (and, for long-distance trips, the airplane), a serious mistake. The Interstate System, with its multilane roadways, elaborate interchanges, bridges and tunnels, is not the only villain, however. Since 1956 the federal government has also helped the states to finance (at a 50-50 ratio) several hundred thousand miles of primary and secondary roads, both urban and rural costing $28 billion. These highways can be just as destructive of cities and countryside as the interstate routes.

City dwellers and homeowners in the path of proposed freeways or adjacent to already constructed highways are not impressed with the economic or social "progress" peddled by highway boosters. They are concerned with the cost in terms of human values, for which there is no price tag. No one has yet devised a method for putting a dollar value on space to live, work, play, and breathe. This concern for human values is especially felt among residents of older cities, which were built long before the advent of the automobile. Freeways do the most damage to these cities. And the Bureau of Public Roads and state highway departments have a long record of ignoring just such concerns, especially when they are expressed at public hearings which are supposed to tell public officials what the community thinks of their proposals. Four-, six-, and eight-lane highways that stretch across the open country providing a link between cities are one thing. But when the same kind of freeway blasts its way into the heart of cities where people live and want to continue to live, the effect is not progress and speed, but destruction.

Freeways isolate nonauto owners, as happened in the Watts district of Los Angeles, where the ghetto area was sealed off by highways. Freeways take living quarters, tightening up an already overburdened housing supply and eating up valuable land, destroying established neighborhoods. Untrammeled freeway construction in urban areas is exacerbating the very crisis in our cities we are hoping to allay. Nowhere has the connection between freeway construction and crisis been more poignantly expressed than in a letter, postmarked Newark, New Jersey, to Daniel Moynihan, then director of the MIT-Harvard Joint Center on Urban Affiars, now Special Assistant to President Nixon on Urban Affairs with cabinet rank, shortly after that city's 1967 riot. Its author pleaded, in part, that "They are tearing down our homes and building up medical colleges (sic) and motor clubs and parking lots and we need decent private homes to live in. They are tearing down our best schools and churches to build a highway. . . ." The evidence is on public record. Michigan Governor George Romney told a Senate committee shortly before his appointment as Secretary of Housing and Urban Development that freeway construction in Detroit was a major cause of that city's 1967 riot.

Besides gobbling up precious land, freeways simply attract more cars into the city, thereby clogging streets so that public transportation, particularly buses, cannot operate efficiently, which in turn results in a decline in passengers, rise in fares and fiscal crises. Urban freeways can only bring automobiles, trucks, and buses into cities. They cannot provide parking spaces for the vehicles they attract, which leads to still another depredation: More and more downtown land is converted to parking space. Nor do freeways stimulate the "dying downtown economy" as Chamber of Commerce and Board of Trade officials would have us believe. Despite massive freeway construction in central business districts of urban areas, retail sales there continue to lose ground to suburban stores, which attract the mushrooming suburban populations. Boston, for instance, lost 9 percent of its total retail sales between 1958 and 1963, despite considerable freeway construction. San Francisco, on the other hand, increased its sales 9 percent during the same period, then halted all freeway construction in 1966. By 1967, sales increased 16 percent over 1963 sales.

At peak hours, the typical urban freeway is clogged with automobiles competing for the same road space, and often, as in the case of the most celebrated Long Island Expressway, cars move bumper to bumper at five miles an hour. Yet an important ingredient in the rationale and justification for building urban freeways is time saved for the commuter. Actually, at peak hours 7:30 to 9:00 A.M. and 4:30 to 6:30 P.M., drivers are likely to be whizzing home on urban expressways at from six to twelve miles per hour. The horse and buggy did as well.

Highway planners respond to such congestion with plans for more lanes of the same or more access or exit ramps. They talk of double-decking lanes of expressways, more tunnels, and bridges. But these new facilities fill up as fast as the concrete hardens. Then the congestion builds up again as more cars are enticed onto the system by the added facilities. More cars enter congested areas, demanding more parking spaces and operating services, all of which take precious and expensive urban land.

In 1966, the Bureau of Public Roads estimated that the federal government was financing to some degree 51,000 miles of highways in our cities alone, and more are planned, to alleviate "urban congestion." Yet, a helicopter trip over any of our major cities quickly demonstrates that our auto traffic problem is not the result of a shortage of streets, but rather, the result of already having too many.

While 5000 miles of interstate freeways have been completed in urban areas, there are 2500 more still to be imbedded in our cities and plans to construct these last miles are meeting stiff opposition from the public. Ironically, these roads are being promoted at the very time 30 percent of the land use in fifty-three central cities in the United States has already been converted to street use. If these cities must continue to absorb more freeway construction, it will mean that their tax bases will be diminished further at the very time our cities are starved for revenue to cope with staggering demands for services. Moreover, these are the most expensive and least economical segments of the Interstate System. New York's most recently proposed Lower Manhattan Expressway was estimated to cost $100 million a *mile*.

While the city resident is slowly squeezed into smaller dwellings, and space for strolling, playing, and shopping diminishes or is carved up by freeways, his counterpart, the commuting suburbanite, trapped in the monopoly of auto transportation, has to maintain two or more cars with the same care and financial commitment he provides his offspring. Furthermore, even suburban commuters are discovering that their cherished quarter acres can be swallowed up by freeway planners. Their land is being taken for widened streets or spurs as the thirst for space to build roads increases. Where once commuters looked on in bewilderment at pickets protesting a freeway through city homes and neighborhoods, today many are inclined to sympathize and even join the protesters because they too are threatened when the highway reaches into their neighborhoods. Suburban housing no longer escapes the path of the freeway any more than central city dwellings. As the burgeoning metropolitan population spreads out—the consequence of beltway and expressway construction—more roads are built to link suburban communities and connect them with the core cities. As a result, suburban Americans spend a great deal of time aimlessly driving around on freeways.

Still, it is the urban portions of the mileage that cause the most serious repercussions, and it is this portion of the Interstate System which was not supposed to be and never should have been built. The standards for the Interstate System are too demanding of land within large cities. The highways are at least four lanes wide. Some are eight and ten lanes wide. This means wide swaths of concrete from 48 to 144 feet, not including footage for dividers, median strips, signs, light poles, and shoulders. A highway this massive can only serve to disrupt the neighborhoods it dissects.

As originally conceived in 1944, the Interstate System was to serve intercity traffic only. It was to serve long-haul traffic and defense purposes. There were to be only spurs from within the cities to connect to the Interstate System, and few of them, not the massive highway construction cities such as Cleveland, Washington, New York, and Chicago have witnessed.

Our motor vehicle traffic was supposed to consist of trucks, buses, and a few interurban private cars. The volumes of automobile traffic we see today were not going to materialize because they were not supposed to be accommodated with all the highways they would need.

But by the end of World War II, highway boosters had decided to make the private automobile the dominant form of urban transportation, and overemphasis on superhighways, particularly Interstate and primary highways, and lack of attention to public transportation left the public with no choice except to drive cars. This multibillion-dollar highway program, so damaging to our cities, is the only means of transportation for most people who drive the same trip in and out of the city each day. Our highway program has, in effect, made it possible for every automobile owner to have his own private transportation system. That meant 86.5 million separate automobile transportation systems in 1969. The average automobile trip is nine miles in length, and most trips occur within a twenty-five-mile radius of metropolitan areas. For such a small area, any other commuting system would have proven more beneficial to the public than our present system of highways which long ago passed the point of efficiency.

The man who promoted the means for financing highways is Representative George Fallon, Democrat, from Maryland. He favored attaching a special purpose tax on gasoline and oil to pay for the system. Unlike other tax revenue, which goes into the general treasury, this tax money goes into a special fund for highway construction only. This elevated the proposal to a self-perpetuating building program and demonstrates how a special purpose tax eternalizes its own use. Critics of the Highway Trust Fund like to point out that if it is justifiable to use gasoline taxes exclusively for highway construction, the federal tax on alcohol should be spent to promote and expand the liquor industry.

At the very time highways were being promoted, public transportation should have been beefed up to provide a more economical means of moving people while demanding less land, money, and waste than expressways, with alternate methods of commuting, such as rapid rail, subways, and improved and express bus service, systems which move large numbers of passengers. The car mania we see around us today would never have developed if people had been provided the sort of public transportation that could have competed successfully with autos and offered our cities truly "balanced" transportation. Instead, by the mid-seventies, the public will have spent more than $50 billion for highways and less than $1 billion for mass transportation. How did we get on this course in the first place?

In 1956, the Federal Highway Act specified that the Interstate System "may be located both in rural and urban areas." It also provided for 90 percent federal financing, an irresistible lure for the politicians, contractors, and state highway officials who wanted as much of the federal pie as possible. Thus it was that expansive freeways through open country were extended into the heart of our major cities. As each new segment of a city's freeway system is completed, it fills up with cars, justifying to highway officials the need for even more of the same. Ironically, the rural portions of the Interstate System cross open land and have little traffic and few lanes. As they approach metropolitan areas, more lanes are added at the very point where land becomes scarce and densely populated.

On the other hand, today's public transportation suffers from freeway construction in several ways that makes it difficult to provide the public with good service that will draw people away from their cars. Bus service is slow because streets are clogged with auto traffic. Then, too the number of transit riders and revenue have traditionally declined in areas where bridges, tunnels, expressways, and parking lots are provided for automobiles, which auto and highway boosters say are the most comfortable and flexible means of transportation. Thus, as profits on public transit nose-dive, equipment deteriorates and service is continually cut back to reduce operating costs. Even such conservative revenue generating measures as fare increases backfire by reducing still further the number of daily riders. Public transportation is in the doldrums while automobile transportation dominates. The outlook for the future is more of the same—only worse.

It is clear that if every commuter to New York City drove in by car, or if the population of Manhattan attempted to travel around town by car, the city would long ago have perished. Yet this has been and is exactly what is being planned in cities across the country. Bureau of Public Roads, state highway officials, and congressmen intend to provide each automobile driver with enough highway facilities to enable him to drive by car anywhere he may wish to go. After the completion date of the present Interstate System, state highway officials have yet another imposing plan waiting in the wings. Among other items, it calls for beefing up the present freeway system in urban areas by building more of them to "relieve" the traffic congestion of the cities!

And they can do it. The Federal Highway Trust Fund collected $5 billion from taxes on gasoline, tires, and auto accessories in 1969. This money, combined with taxes collected by the states, amounts to a $15-billion-a-year-road-building operation. That large an inducement is hard to resist. Add a dash of the strong lobbying from trucking and auto interests on Congress and the public ends up with a massive road-building program.

To appreciate the magnitude of the U.S. road-building and automobile complex, one need only study Detroit's own figures. In 1969, according to statistics issued by the Automobile Manufacturers Association, automotive retail sales, including passenger car, bus and truck, totaled $62 billion, double the figure in 1958. Sales figures for tires, batteries, gasoline and accessories totaled $30 billion. This amount, coupled with the $15 billion road-building operation, plus the cost for insurance, driver education and parking expenses, brings the total bill for motor vehicle transportation to over $120 billion per year.

We spent $35.8 billion in 1969 for grades kindergarten through twelve in our public school system and $61.4 billion for *all* education in the United States. Thus we are spending twice as much on automobile transportation as on all forms of education. Education, however, must vie among the country's list of priorities for its funds, while highways are assured a steady inflow of cash to the Trust Fund.

Detroit's figures ensure a rosy future for auto manufacturers. From their point of view, a $15-billion-annual-road-building project, financed by the taxpayer himself, provides the system so necessary for the increased use of their products. Detroit's optimism is well reflected in a 1966 statement by Lynn Townsend, chairman of the Chrysler Corporation, in which he said:

> The same powerful forces that have created the steadily growing demand for cars over the past five years will continue to operate in the years ahead. These forces include the steady growth of the population and the addition each year of millions of potential new customers, the rise in personal income, and the increasing reliance upon the automobile for personal transportation. In the early 1970's we expect these forces to create a yearly demand ranging between 9 and 12 million new cars.

Mr. Townsend might have mentioned forces more powerful than the population growth or rising personal income (auto prices increase each year too) which operate to "increase reliance upon the automobile for personal transportation." These forces are the auto manufacturers themselves, labor unions, engineers, road contractors, truckers, steel, rubber and petroleum producers, busline and highway officials, and congressmen who protect and parcel out the Highway Trust Fund, from which the 90-10 bounty flows.

One fifth of all steel produced is sold for automobiles and highway construction. It is steel's biggest market. Two thirds of all rubber produced ends up on America's highways, and nine tenths of all gasoline, the petroleum industry's major product, is burned up there, too. In fact, as the Ethyl Corporation tells it, 130,000 gallons of gasoline are consumed every minute by motor vehicles, most of which are automobiles. Americans use twenty-three times more gasoline for individual transportation than any other national group. As for auto manufacturers, they watch their sales fluctuate as a mother watches a feverish child's temperature. They sold 8.8 million private automobiles with a dollar value of $19.2 billion in 1968 when private car registration exceeded 84 million.

The construction and related industries have a stake in the program, too. In 1961, it was estimated that every million dollars of highway construction bought 16,800 barrels of cement, 694 tons of bituminous material, 485 tons of concrete and clay pipe, 76,000 tons of sand, gravel, slag, stone, and other mineral materials, 24,000 pounds of explosives, 121,000 gallons of petroleum products, 99,000 feet of lumber, and 600 tons of steel. Multiply those amounts by 15 thousand to equal the $15 billion spent on highway construction in 1967.

The taxpayer plays his role, too, by footing the bill. The only difference is that he has no control over where the money will be spent or where the roads will be built. Moreover, today, the fact that a motorist can drive on our highway system is less the result of an attempt to provide transportation than it is a side benefit of highway construction undertaken for construction's sake and insured automobile sales.

Highway boosters have attempted to make highways answer all of our transportation needs. In 1954, two years before passage of the 1956 Highway Act and establishment of the Highway Trust Fund, there were 9.4 million trucks on all United States public roads hauling 213 billion ton miles of products. (A ton mile is one ton of cargo transported one mile.) By 1966, there were 14.7 million trucks hauling more than 400 billion tons miles between urban areas. The industry has almost doubled in size and service.

The truckers boast that they are moving goods across the nation in tones that suggest that railroads do not exist and are not doing the same job. Automobile ads tell us that car dealers are matchmakers. Highway officials argue that they are for a "balanced transportation system," which means that they will support mass transit construction as long as they can build all the highways they wish. If the congressional guardians of the Highway Trust Fund truly believed in providing transportation, they would be willing to allow trust fund money to finance whichever mode of transportation a community chose. Instead, they shout that highway taxes are collected to build highways only and that the motoring public is paying for more of them, not subway systems or any other form of transportation. Worst of all, the promoters of more roads claim that the system works, when in fact it does so in cities only in the wee small hours of the morning when practically no one is driving. The rush hour is the very time the system is supposed to work and also the very time when it most often breaks down. The highway promoters' answer to this criticism is that the traffic congestion only proves the need for still *more* highways.

For years, highway officials have touted the economic desirability of automobile travel and safety. Today they are more cautious about claiming that driving saves money, but they still cry "safety" when someone criticizes a new freeway. They do not mention that automobile accidents are maiming three million, costing billions in damages and killing more than 55,000 Americans each year. The National Safety Council estimates that more Americans have been killed by automobiles than in all of the wars this country has fought. Yet hungry highway promoters dismiss these statistics as inevitable consequences of our "culture."

Apparently our culture promotes the idea that it is healthy, safe, wise, and economical to fill our large cities every morning with serpentine streams of automobiles whose drivers again each evening wend their weary way out. Apparently our culture, aware that the average automobile carries 1.6 persons per trip and that thus less than 5000 people can travel a single lane of freeway in one hour, while a double-track rail system can move 50,000 in the same time, still prefers the smell of exhaust fumes and the interminable wait in traffic jams.

As former Secretary of Transportation Alan Boyd so aptly stated, during his brief tenure in office, "If someone were to tell you he had seen strings of noxious gases drifting among the buildings of a city, black smoke blotting out the sun, great holes in the major streets, filled with men in hard hats, planes circling overhead, unable to land, and thousands of people choking the streets, pushing and shoving in a desperate effort to get out of the city . . . you would be hard pressed to know whether he was talking about a city at war or a city at rush hour."

Since by 1975 the population may be 215 million and forecasters predict that there will be 98.5 million automobiles on the road, possibly every other man, woman, and child will be operating an automobile by then. The question is where? If the major growth in population occurs in our urban areas and the automobile remains the predominant method of transportation, all of our large city centers will be huge concrete slabs with office buildings interspersed among parking lots and freeways, washed daily by the exhaust fumes of masses of internal combustion engines. Even if the much touted cleaner operating electric car becomes practical for inner-city travel, it will still not solve our traffic and parking difficulties. For while air pollution is an undesirable by-product of our expressway systems, ultimately it is the space which the system occupies that becomes crucial in any economic appraisal.

This space included not only the very ground, river, or gorge upon or through which the road is constructed, but also the space needed for parking and interchanges and ramps to get on and off the freeway. It doesn't end there. The space next to the freeway is also affected. Sometimes it is isolated by the freeway, such as an expressway running along a riverfront which cuts off access to the water, which might have been used as a means of transportation itself (to say nothing of what it does to the view). A highway can cause repercussions if it takes other facilities such as schools, churches, homes, stores, or parks. A loss of one or all of these facilities can mean a squeezing together or doubling up of remaining like facilities. One less house or school can overcrowd another house or school which attempts to absorb the people displaced by the highway. And there is no guarantee that the highway will actually facilitate transportation.

During off-peak hours some urban freeways can work relatively well, providing motor vehicles with a comfortable and quick system for moving around, another plus for highways. But come 5 P.M. on any weekday, millions of perfectly normal, happy, intelligent Americans become snarling, aggressive, frustrated, or defeated human beings as they vie for road space with their fellow drivers. Not particularly because they choose to do so, but because they have been provided roads to drive everywhere and few suitable alternatives. What happens when commuters, wedded to the idea of driving their automobiles to work daily, are offered a quality alternative?

Special efforts must be made to draw these commuters away from their cars, but the task is not an impossible one. A Housing and Urban Development sponsored demonstration project in Peoria, Illinois, during 1965, which provided a "premium" bus service for factory employees, enticed regular auto drivers onto a special door-to-work bus service. Significantly, free auto parking spaces were available for all employees at each factory location.

Yet 542 commuters chose the bus service. They reported that they felt relaxed and comfortable riding the bus, that it was cheaper than driving a car to work, and that it was prompt and reliable. Equally important, the service proved to be profitable for the bus company.

Some passengers even sold their second car when they learned that the experimental bus service was to become a permanent operation of the local bus company, a relatively positive consumer endorsement for an alternative to automobile transportation.

A significant number of people were lured away from their automobiles even when the service operated in territory served by regular buses, which they could have been but were not using to make the trip to work. The difference was that the premium bus service took passengers from their individual front doors to work in the morning and back in the evening. Twenty-eight percent of the premium bus service passengers were former regular bus riders who switched, but the remaining 72 percent represented a new market of former automobile users. Thus, for every regular passenger the bus company lost to premium service, it gained three new customers.

Michael Blurton, director of the bus project for the University of Illinois, said such a premium bus service could be adapted to larger cities, and he suggests they can be incorporated into a rapid-rail or subway system to pick up commuters at their door and deposit them at the rail or subway line.

Theoretically, if many auto drivers would use this bus service, there would be fewer cars using Peoria's streets and highways during peak traffic hours, the traffic situation would ease, and it would be possible for the highways to operate efficiently. Fewer cars on the streets would make it easier for trucks to make deliveries and buses to pick up and discharge passengers. There would be no pressing need for additional highways.

Although highway systems in our large cities ceased long ago to provide efficient transportation, the American taxpayer keeps on paying good money to have his cities torn up and paved over. The National Planning Association estimates that by 1975, 164 million people will be living in the nation's 224 metropolitan areas. The association further predicts that 60 percent or almost 100 million of these urban dwellers will live in the 25 largest urban areas. Thus it is expected that each of these 25 cities will have an average population of 4 million by 1975. Clearly, all available space in these 25 areas will be fully taxed to provide services the burgeoning populations will demand. But what services? Facilities for automobile travel?

In 1968, there were 100 million motor vehicles operating on public roads. Of that number, 84 million were private automobiles. By 1975, it is estimated that there will be 118 million motor vehicles, 98.5 million of which will be automobiles. The estimate surely will prove correct by 1975 if highway promoters provide the freeways and parking spaces for these automobiles and if our lungs can survive ever increasing air pollution.

To avoid this onslaught of more automobiles, we must stop building freeways and obliging automobile traffic in areas of dense population. We must stop listening to engineers and highway planners, men who explain the effects of displacing people and services in very vague terms. Even more vague, in the mind of the highway planner, at least, is the direct social or economic effect of taking a park or wildlife refuge for highway use. Since highway designers and planners equate cost-benefit in terms of dollar value, it becomes a sticky problem to measure the utility of, say, a public golf course or a bird sanctuary. But they have been convinced in the past that they could prove such public land is less valuable than a highway which destroys it.

Else why would the state and federal highway officials approve a plan to construct a freeway like the North Expressway through the historic city of the Alamo, San Antonio? The center of this city enjoys a park and natural landscape complex virtually downtown which consists of open spaces, college campuses, a river, zoo, golf course, and a flood basin. Now let's see what the highway planners designed for this Texas city.

As proposed, the expressway is to curve and wind its way across an Audubon bird sanctuary and Olmos Creek, a tributary in its natural state which would be converted into a concrete ditch, on along a picnic ground and recreation area, wiping out a Girl Scout Day Camp and nature trail, rise across the Olmos basin to the height of the Olmos Dam, where it would cross, sever a college campus, force an elementary school to close, pass through the zoo, block off the public gymnasium, follow the edge of the sunken gardens, past the outdoor theatre where it squeezed between this and the municipal school stadium, blocking a major entrance, entered residential San Antonio, taking homes, swiping off part of a municipal golf course, and limp home through a wooded portion of the San Antonio River's natural watercourse, one of the few remaining wilderness areas left in the city.

This is a classic example of highway planning. In other cities with expressway controversies, the fight has centered on demolition of a park or disruption of a neighborhood or the severing of a campus or the bisecting of a zoo or of a golf course or the loss of a school or treasured trees. Here, San Antonio has the dubious distinction of falling victim to all of the typical hazards of highway planning. Clearly, the planners of San Antonio's North Expressway did not know where NOT to build. It was only after years of pressure from numerous citizen groups that the Bureau and state highway officials agreed in 1969 to consider tunneling portions of the expressway. At this writing no commitment has been made to tunnel, however.

In late 1966, the same year the North Expressway was proposed for San Antonio, the Bureau of Public Roads back in Washington issued a report for fiscal 1966 called "Highways and Human Values." An introduction to the report stated:

While the social responsibilities inherent in highway construction have

always been recognized by the Bureau of Public Roads and the State
Highway Departments, no 12 month period has produced more
accomplishments toward making our highways serve many public needs
other than transportation. Nor has any comparable period yielded
greater results in the important fields of highway safety and esthetics.

The year was characterized by new emphasis on the total impact of
highways on people—on their environment, housing, recreation, cultural
interests, and all the other elements of life in the complex latter half of
the 20th century.

Some new social ideas emerge in connection with the highway
program, but 1966 was probably more notable for the coming of age of
concepts dating back several years or even decades.

. . . the need for greater attention to those aspects involving more
than getting the motorist and trucker from here to there became
increasingly apparent and the Federal-State highway partnership began
devoting a much greater share of its time and talent to the human
values involved in the Interstate and other Federal-aid highway
programs.

Apparently the author hadn't heard of San Antonio's North Expressway.
Few freeway proposals will do more damage to environment, housing,
recreation, and cultural interests than the expressway as originally scheduled
for that delightful Texas city in 1966. Where is the federal-state highway
partnership which the report assured us was even then devoting a much
greater share of its time and talent to the human values involved in the
hishway program?

Almost three years after those pious words appeared in the 1966 report,
Edward "Ted" Holmes, for many years the brains behind the planning of
Bureau of Public Roads at the federal level, stated that the north leg of
Washington's proposed inner loop should be placed "along R or S Street off
Connecticut Avenue. That area east of Connecticut could use some
redevelopment. It's a pretty grubby area."

That "grubby area" is my neighborhood. It contains deteriorating houses.
It also contains renovated houses, and the neighborhood boasts an intergrated
population of sophisticated city dwellers. Numerous national associations and
embassies occupy stately mansions among our tree-lined streets, and the area
contains excellent Spanish, French, Japanese, Mexican, and American
restaurants and numerous small businesses and shops and well as spiffy
boutiques along Connecticut Avenue. The proposed freeway would isolate or
obliterate many brownstones and mansions such as the former home of the
Willard family, founders of the Willard Hotel, the house where Daniel Chester
French lived and designed the Lincoln Memorial, numerous pre-Civil War
houses, and a tiny farmhouse that was, in its day, on the outskirts of the
nation's capital. It would also slice through an elementary school district
which parents and community people recently fought hard to acquire as a
community-controlled school.

In other words, the north leg would wipe out the core of this
neighborhood of people redevelop the blight that exists in the area. Yet, time
and time again, such freeway construction is peddled as redevelopment and
progress. It was the specter of just such redevelopment in the form of the

north leg freeway cutting through our living room which sparked my interest in expressways back in 1965. I soon found that there were others in the District of Columbia who were fighting proposed freeway systems.

Repeated sorties into the D.C. Highway Department's logic for building freeways in the nation's capital produced ever mounting evidence that such a system would not address itself to the city's transportation crisis. In addition, poll after poll of residents of the District revealed overwhelming opposition to any more road building, and by 1966 suburbanites were expressing a greater interest in beginning a fledgling rapid transit as an alternative to roads. Undaunted, highway planners pressed on, bulldozing churches, schools, houses, and parkland.

10

The "Cinderella" of the Cities: Urban Mass Transit

As the problems of the urban expressways became ever more pronounced, public attention began to turn to what planning expert Thomas E. Lisco called the new "Cinderella" of the cities—mass transit. Yet as his timely essay in 1969 illustrates, the problems confronting the new panacea of urban transportation were staggering. It would be difficult to lure the American away from his private automobile; only by combining convenience, low cost and luxury would mass transit truly succeed. If transit officials could not deliver on these basic considerations then, like the earlier Cinderella of the 1950s, the expressways, mass transit would turn into a pumpkin. The director of Research of the Chicago Area Transportation Study, Mr. Lisco's observations of 1969 remain valid for the mid-seventies.

Document†

Urban mass transportation in the United States is in the early stages of a vast transformation, a transformation that will rival the rags-to-riches change visited upon a fairy tale Cinderella.

There is little question about the rags part of the statement. Mass transportation in the United States can aptly and generally be characterized as dirty, run-down, and financially strapped. It is suffering large deficits and has lost more than half its patronage in the last twenty years. The larger the system, the larger the deficit and the more critical the situation; in New York City the deficit on operations alone was over $50 million in fiscal 1968 with 1969 projections of $150 million. Similar statements can be made about commuter railroads. Deficits abound, systems are run-down and dirty, and stepping into a present-day commuter railroad car is often like entering a museum piece of the nineteenth century.

But riches? Oddly, that is also true. One might think that the consistent failure of mass transportation to hold its own over more than two decades indicates its lack of economic rationale, and thus suggests an imminent and appropriate demise. But the fact remains that mass transportation arteries are as important to the well-being of our cities as express highways. Because mass transportation performs a vital economic function, not only for the

†From: Thomas E. Lisco, *The Public Interest*, Number 18 (Winter 1970), 52-74. Copyright © by National Affairs, Inc., 1970; 3.

individuals who use it, but also for the very form and efficiency of the city, it *must* be made to succeed. Further, there are forces now at work that may help ensure this success.

THE RATIONAL COMMUTER. To understand mass transportation—its problems and possibilities—requires understanding of its most important customer, the commuter.

The typical urban American's conversation about getting to work follows a predictable pattern beginning with a long monologue that indicates exactly how he saves time getting to work. If he drives, he knows all the tricks. He times traffic signals to the second, follows special routes at different times of the day, and he has pinpointed the location of every speed trap. Altogether, he has carefully thought through the task of getting to work in order not to lose a second's time. He has made an exact science of commuting. A second monologue follows this one and it concerns the others on the highways. What a bunch of idiots they are! Why do they insist on congesting "my" road, and, for heaven's sake, why don't they use mass transportation? It is perfectly clear to the speaker that he uses his automobile for good reasons, but the others who drive must be irrational and peculiar. Their only motive for driving surely must be a totally irrational "love affair" with the car.

If our conversationalist happens to go to work by mass transportation, he, too, has worked his trip out to the smallest detail. He knows the minute he must leave home in order to catch his bus or train. He also knows where to stand in order to catch the car that offers the greatest likelihood of finding a seat, or lets him off nearest his exit at the station. Railroad commuters are known to sit in the same seat of the same car each day, and to be highly resentful when ill-informed interlopers take "their" places.

If the auto driver outraged by the others who use the roads, the train commuter is bewildered by them. How can people choose to fight expressway congestion, to breathe fumes and build up nervous tension, when they could use mass transportation? The commuter rail traveler sits in his train comfortably reading the paper, while drivers are stuck in unmoving lines of cars on the expressway. Because he generally gets to work faster than if he drove, the auto driver's choice seems senseless to him.

In fact, however, both decisions make sense. Commuters are just as careful in choosing their mode of travel as they are in calculating strategy for the interior portion of their trip. Indeed, it would be odd if they decided their mode of travel off-handedly, and then calculated minor maneuvers to the second.

As one might expect, the basic decision between using the automobile or using mass transportation depends on the relative times, relative costs, and relative levels of comfort and convenience offered by the competing travel modes. Generally, rapid transit and commuter railroads are cheaper than automobiles, and permit the use of the family car by other members of the household. On the other hand, automobiles go virtually any place, at any time. They do not require adherence to a schedule.

In two other aspects mass transportation can sometimes be superior, though sometimes inferior, to driving. One is comfort. Because they are modern, clean, and air-conditioned, as well as involving less strain than driving in heavy traffic, some commuter railroads offer more comfort than automobiles. On the other hand, standing in a crowded car for the entire trip on a rapid vehicle may make heavy traffic driving a good deal more appealing. Traffic moves slowly, but at least automobile commuters are seated.

Relative travel times can also favor either mass transportation or automobile. For particular destinations—notably those in the downtown areas of large cities—overall mass transportation travel times may compare very favorably with those of automobiles. For travel between outlying areas of cities, however, mass transportation rarely competes with the automobile. Frequently, direct public transportation lines do not exist. In such cases, mass transportation simply does not provide an alternative to driving.

It is the sum of these calculations that dictates the individual's choice. For some, one aspect may be particularly important, while for others, another may carry disproportionate weight. But overall, there is a remarkable consistency in the response to the alternatives presented. Where mass transportation is a good alternative to driving, people use mass transportation. Where it is not, they drive.

PATTERNS OF CHOICES. Because commuters make consistent and rational decisions on their modes of travel, the patterns of automobile and mass transportation use across cities are clear. Thus, for travel between outlying areas and downtown—where mass transportation is competitive in time and cost with driving—use of transit and commuter rail lines is heavy. In Chicago, for example, fully 87 per cent of the people going to the downtown area during the morning rush period get there by commuter railroad or transit. Of the remaining 13 per cent who drive, about half do so only because they need their cars during the day. In New York, the relative proportions are even more extreme. There is no mystery to this. In Chicago, rush hour driving to and from downtown is difficult, and "Loop" parking costs are high. Mass transit and commuter rail services are both good. In New York, the mass transit and commuter rail services are even more comprehensive than Chicago's and driving at rush hour is impossible. That few people drive is a foregone conclusion.

In cities with less developed downtown areas, lower parking costs, less highway congestion, and smaller transit systems, automobile driving to central areas comprises a much greater proportion of the travel that is directed downtown. The relative costs and benefits favor highways, and commuters respond by driving.

The patterns are very different for travel between areas that are not downtown. The available mass transportation service is usually restricted to buses, which are rarely time competitive with automobiles because they use the same right of way and make stops. In costs, peripheral travel also favors the automobile. Because parking is available and cheap (mostly free) outside of downtown, automobile costs remain near operating costs. These costs are close to those of mass transportation.

The results are clear. Because peripheral travel is more favorable to automobiles than is downtown travel, both in elapsed travel time and in cost, the actual proportion of travel by mass transportation on the periphery is much smaller than that to downtown. In fact, while all segments of the population use mass transportation for downtown travel, peripheral mass transportation mainly serves persons who cannot drive or afford cars, or who have limited access to them.

THE KEY TO SUCCESS: DEMAND. If relative times, costs, and comfort are crucial to commuters, passenger volumes are critical to mass transportation operations. Whether it be rail rapid transit or commuter railroad, mass transportation cannot exist unless it carries a very large number of passengers. The absolute lower limit for economic investment in surface rail routes is about 5,000 passengers a day, while that for a subway is in the vicinity of 40,000.

These lower limits determine directly where transit and commuter rail lines can and cannot be built. They almost automatically rule out successful rail transit in metropolitan areas of less than a million inhabitants. Cities below this threshold-size simply do not have corridors generating enough travel demand to make commuter railroads or rail rapid transit a good investment. However, even in cities with populations well over a million, mass transportation cannot be a substitute for highways or an instant panacea for transportation problems. Even cities as large as Chicago, Philadelphia, San Francisco, and Boston generate enough traffic to support rail transportation lines only in certain corridors. In all of these cities, the only type of rail transportation that can economically survive is the type that serves travel demands from outlying areas to the city center. Demand for other kinds of travel is simply too diffuse to support rail lines. With present-day technology, such demands can economically be served only by highways.

In certain other cities, also well above the 1 million threshold, even such central-area-serving lines are not assured of economic success. In Washington, D.C., with a metropolitan area population of over 2 million persons, laws restricting the heights of downtown buildings have made the central area so diffuse that the possibilities for economically visable rail transportation are greatly limited. Los Angeles is similar. It is difficult even to find a real"downtown" in Los Angeles.

The only city in the United States that has the density to support a general crosshatching of rail transit routes is New York. The travel demands in all directions are so incredible, over a large area, that parrallel rail transit lines can exist only blocks away from one another. There is no other city in the United States, however, in which this condition is presently approached or is likely to be approached in the near future.

SUPPLY: A KEY TO THE SHAPE OF A CITY. The law of threshold demand for rail transportation lines determines where such lines can succeed. This law, however, has an important converse. Just as rapid transit and commuter railroads cannot exist without high trip-making density, so high trip-making density cannot exist without rapid transit and commuter railroads. Cities such as New York and Chicago simply could not support the economic activities of their central areas without rapid transit and commuter railroads.

As before, the reason narrows down to travel volumes. When volumes of travel are high, rail mass transportation lines can do jobs that highways cannot even attempt. Again, consider the actual numbers. In Chicago, during the three quarter-hour period between 4:45 P.M. and 5:30 P.M., the six rail transit lines and eight commuter railroads carry nearly 120,000 passengers away from the downtown area. Carrying this many persons in the same time by automobile, with typically existing passenger loads per car, would require 70 express highway lanes. Chicago is already thought to be well supplied with express highways, having 29 limited access lanes leading out from downtown. The addition of another 70 would just about blanket the inner city. In New York, the idea of doing the mass transportation job with highways is even more ludicrous. Commuter rail lines and transit carry more than 1.3 million passengers to and from jobs in midtown Manhattan every day. This job just could not be done with automobiles.

The implications of these figures are dramatic. Plainly stated, if a city wishes to have a well-developed and dense downtown area, it must have high-volume transportation lines to serve that area. The downtowns of Detroit and Los Angeles have been hurt for years because those cities have no rail transportation routes serving downtown. Chicago, Boston, Philadelphia, and New York all have such transportation facilities, and all have been experiencing tremendous building booms in their downtown areas during the postwar years. Perhaps the most dramatic indication of the effects of mass transportation facilities is seen in those cities that did not possess a rail transit system, but have recently built one or are presently doing so. In Toronto, an unparalleled building boom along Yonge Street coincided with the construction of the Yonge Street subway line. This one line completely altered the focus of the central area of the city. Previously concentrated around Queen and Yonge, new high-rise developments have sprung up outside the central core at key stations of the subway.

In San Francisco, the construction of the Bay Area Rapid Transit System is causing a similar transformation to take place on Market Street. This street of recently-faded elegance is currently experiencing a resurgence that will shortly make it regain its place as the most successful commercial street in the city. The cause: a rapid transit system that will not even carry its first passenger for another two years.

Montreal is yet another example of the tremendous response of real estate values to improved mass transportation facilities. There, too, the spectacular growth of the downtown area is associated with construction of a new mass transportation system.

All of these examples illustrate the close relation between the shape of the city and the capabilities of its transportation system. Just as early railway lines dictated the locations of city suburbs 150 years ago, the placements of highways and mass transportation lines mold cities today. For the most part, in our larger cities, this means high-volume transportation lines serving the city center and express highways serving the rest of the city as well as the downtown area. In some cases, there are no high-density travel facilities. In those cases the center of the city is badly hurt by that lack. In the case of New York City the whole inner city is so dense that within Manhattan only a small fraction of the transportation job is done by highways. But now, as in the past, the relation between dense travel needs and high-volume travel arteries holds. Cities with high-density cores have transportation systems capable of handling high-density travel. Conversely, cities without high-density travel transportation systems cannot have high-density cores.

There is, then, an economic rationale for an appropriate mix of mass transportation and highway facilities in our large urban areas. It is also evident that commuters make logical, reasonable, and largely predictable choices of transportation modes for accomplishing their various trips. Further, these reasonable choices of travel modes indicate the types of travel needs that should be served by highways and the types that should be served by rapid transit systems and commuter railroads. What has yet to be shown is the reason why, in spite of economic rationality and indeed utter economic necessity, the rapid transit systems and commuter railroads of this country have generally performed so miserably in the postwar years. Presumably, where there is economic necessity, and particularly where there is a natural monopoly, there is money to be made. However, this natural monopoly has conspicuously not made money nor broken even. Why not?

There are a number of reasons that tend to be somewhat different for rapid transit systems than for commuter railroads. Similarities outweigh dissimilarities, however, and the changes that will revolutionize both commuter railroads and transit systems will be remarkably alike.

THE PROBLEMS OF TRANSIT SYSTEMS. The crux of the transit problem can be summed up in two words: comfort and price. There is a somewhat peculiar notion held by many that the modern urban American should be delighted to use mass transit—*any* mass transit—simply because it is cheaper than driving. The overwhelming contrary evidence provided by the amount of highway travel in our cities confuses these people who regard such behavior as economically irrational. Further, they blame this "irrationality" for creating the commuting problem.

On the contrary, it is preposterous to expect anyone with reasonable income, attractive home, and air-conditioned office, to submit to rush hour jostling, crowding, and standing in transit cars that combine inadequate heating and nonexistent air-conditioning with poor riding characteristics. People willing to pay a high premium for their comfrot at home and in the office, will pay just as much for comfort traveling between them. And when they are faced with the choice between being herded like cattle into a rush-hour transit vehicle, or driving a well-engineered, quiet, and comfortable automobile, the decision is an easy one in spite of additional expense. In fact, only exorbitant parking costs and extreme traffic congestion can guarantee the continued voluntary use of run-down and unattractive transit.

The second reason for transit difficulties—and ultimately the more important one—lies in pricing. The pricing policies of our transit systems could hardly be worse. Not only are fares set at levels that virtually guarantee that transit companies will teeter on the edge of bankruptcy, but they are set with little regard for the most elementary principles of economics.

THE PRICE LEVEL. The major pricing problem results from the fact that almost universally *the fares charged on rapid transit systems in the United States are not too high—they are too low.* For political and other reasons, transit fares are consistently maintained at levels below those necessary for economic operation. The results are disastrous. Faced with persistent shortages of cash, the transit companies are simply unable to function properly. They are unable to provide modern equipment; they are unable to maintain structures and roadways; they are unable to provide protection against crime for the passengers on their property; they are unable to support proper research facilities; they are unable to provide good service. In short, they are not able to perform adequately any of the necessary and normal functions of an up-to-date industry operating in a technologically advanced society.

At first glance, placing the blame for this multitude of problems on the level of the transit fare alone seems an unwarranted, and simplistic response to an extremely complex situation. To challenge such a bold statement of causation, one might be tempted to ask some of the following questions:

1. If fares were actually raised to "economic" levels, how high would they be? A dollar for a trip at present costing twenty-five or thirty cents?

2. How can higher fares answer the problems of transit when the usual postwar pattern has been price rises that lead to less patronage, followed by cuts in service that lead to higher prices, etc.? Can this vicious spiral have any end other than the ultimate bankruptcy of the transit company?

3. If prices are raised to "economic" levels, how will it be possible to provide cheap transportation for the poor people who need it most?

4. Finally, isn't transit inherently *uneconomic* because much of the equipment must necessarily lie idle—and not earning revenue—during most of the day?

Each of these questions is reasonable on the surface, but each illustrates one of the common mass transportation myths. Let us consider them in order.

1. *The incredibly high fare myth.* Rapid transit fares must generally be higher—considerably higher than at present—if the transit industry is to provide the type of transportation that a modern society demands. In absolute terms, however, the necessary price rises are not very large.

Suppose a transit company raises the fare from twenty-five to forty cents. For the great majority of individuals, this extra fifteen cents per ride is not very significant. To the transit company, however, such a fare increase may be very important. Even given the usual patronage response to transit fare increases, this 60 percent price rise should add to total revenue about 40 percent.

For most transit companies such large revenue increases are particularly important and can represent the difference between chronic cash shortages and enough revenue both to allow good service and to encourage investment capital. . . .

Fares of a dollar for transit? Given their monopoly position, some companies could conceivably charge that fare and make an exorbitant profit. But operating a transit system is just not that expensive except for unusually long trips. Much more modest fares can assure both deficit-free operation for the present and a solid financial base for the future.

2. *The price-patronage-service-spiral myth.* This myth has its roots in the mistaken assignment of a causal relation between two largely independent postwar changes in urban transit. One, a secular change from lower to higher fares; the other, a dramatic decline in the use of certain types of transit, attended by corresponding service reductions.

Although changes in fare levels have had some influence in determining transit use, their role has actually been quite minor. The automobile has been a much more powerful determinant. The great change in the use of mass transportation since World War II was almost entirely the result of the new availability of cheap and convenient automobiles, and of the advent of urban expressways. During World War II, whether convenient or not, mass transportation had to be used because of gasoline rationing. During the decade of the Great Depression, only a small proportion of the population could afford automobiles. Of course, at no time until after the war did more than a very few urban expressways exist. The result was that, after the war, the change in auto ownership that normally would have been spread over several decades, actually took place in little more than one. At the same time, a massive urban expressway building program took place. The overall consequence of this dual development was that suddenly the bulk of the population was provided with a relatively cheap and very convenient means of transportation that it had never before possessed. Correspondingly, the mass transit and commuter rail companies found their role rather abruptly changed from that of providing most urban transportation services, to that of providing only those services that could compete with the automobile.

Where did the changes take place? Not surprisingly, travel *not* directed toward central areas was particularly affected, especially bus transportation. In the decade following World War II, bus use in major metropolitan areas dropped by roughly a third. The drop in transit use took place just exactly where the automobile could best compete.

At the same time, however rail transit use to and from central areas fell much less. The slow fall in such transit use continued until the early 1960's when the trend changed to what has been a continuing moderate *increase*. Again, the change was what one would expect. Where rapid transit can compete with automobiles, routes on exclusive rights of way providing competitive travel times to areas with high parking costs, the advent of mass automobile transportation has had only a minor effect. Now that almost all people who want automobiles can have them, the normal process of growth in population and travel is reasserting itself in increased rail transit use.

Why have fare changes played only a minor role? Because other criteria influence choices between travel modes. Variables such as parking costs, relative travel times, and comfort of the transit fare. Parking costs of two dollars a day at a given downtown destination clearly must dwarf the effects of a ten-or fifteen-cent transit fare rise on travel mode choices. . . . Generally, differences in elapsed times between travel modes . . . can vary by twenty minutes, a half hour, or more. The effects of these differences between travel modes minimize those of potential fare changes. Finally, as indicated above, if comfort can have value measured in dollars per trip, then the actual transit fare becomes relatively insignificant. An unpleasant transit ride at a quarter is just as unpleasant at thirty-five cents.

A price-patronage-service-spiral does *not* represent reality in rapid transit. The role that transit plays in serving the transportation needs of a city depends far more on the nature of the city and of the transit system, than on the fare. If transit is comfortable and convenient, people will use it either at an economic fare or at an artificially low one. Otherwise, they will use it only' if they have to. But either way, the amount of the fare will have only a marginal effect on the use of the system.

3.*The cheap transit myth: who pays and who benefits?* The cheap transportation myth is the most unfortunate of all the myths associated with mass transit because the policies that come from it have results exactly opposite to those intended. Virtually the only rationale offered for maintaining transit fares below market levels is to provide cheap transportation for poor people. In fact, what we do through artificially keeping fares low is to cause tremendous underinvestment returns low or negative, it is exceedingly difficult to attract investment to mass transportation. The result is not cheap transit, but, for many, no transit at all. . . .

The major effect of low fares is lack of public transportation, but there is another implication of the low-fare theory that is just as perverse. Although most persons favoring cheap transportation for the poor specify not only that it be cheap, but also that it be of high quality, in actuality this turns out not to be the case. Cheap transportation for poor people almost invariably means poor transportation for poor people. In reality the poor are forced to submit to discomfort and bad service, while the rich drive their automobiles. . . .

The final blow to the cheap transit for poor people policy is a standard economic argument. If subsidization of transportation for the poor is an appropriate public policy, then why not do it directly? Why should all persons using transit be subsidized with scarce public resources to help the few who actually need subsidy? Indiscriminate subsidization of all for the benefit of the few is an extremely expensive type of public aid. . . .

By its very nature, mass transportation will always be cheap transportation. Economics dictates that moving people in groups measured in hundreds costs less than moving them in groups of two or three. However, only if we charge for transit what transit costs can provide cheap and good transportation—for all the people.

4.*The inherent diseconomies myth.* This myth is included so often in discussions of mass transit that it should finally be laid to rest. The argument states that the extreme "peaking" characteristics of transit demand—high demand at rush hour, low demand otherwise—means transit vehicles cannot pay their way. Transit cars cannot work enough hours during the day to make their use economical. Such is the argument.

Does constancy of use really determing value? Are restaurants "inherently diseconomic" because they are busy only at meal times? Are ski resorts poor investments because they are used only for a few months during the year? Clearly, these enterprises can be perfectly good investments. Transit is the same. Whether any of these investments provides a good return on capital depends, not on the evenness of demand, but rather on the relation between the demand for the service and the costs of supplying that demand. In the transit industry there are many places where demand for the service is more than enough to justify providing the supply.

The Price Structure   The pricing problems of transit begin with the overall levels of fares. Unfortunately, they do not end there. Problems of inappropriate internal fare structures plague the industry, compounding the difficulties already caused by artificially low overall prices.

The crux of the internal price-structure problem lies in the single fare system. The majority of our mass transit systems charge the same amount for six blocks or sixteen miles. This is economically inefficient because it automatically requires that short trips subsidize long ones. Because the fare is set near the average cost of providing service both for long and for short trips, the persons making short trips pay more than it costs the transit company to provide the service, while those taking long trips pay less. . . .

Many trips that would be economically worthwhile at a fare approximating the cost of providing the service are frequently not worthwhile at that cost *plus* the price of subsidizing longer trips. For example, a six-block trip on existing service may well be worthwhile at the twenty-five-cent cost of providing that service, but not at the average forty cents per ride cost of operating the entire transit system. Therefore, persons who would potentially use transit for short trips walk or use other modes of transportation. For no good economic reason, short trips are priced both above their cost and above their value to potential transit riders, thus causing losses to all concerned.

While the single fare system causes the transit user to suffer only when contemplating a short trip, the transit company loses on both types of trip. Not only does it lose revenue by overpricing short trips but by underpricing long ones as well. Just as it costs more to provide transportation for long trips than for short ones, that transportation is correspondingly worth more to the persons who wish to use it. Therefore, if transit companies used rational pricing policies, they would charge higher fares for longer trips. Unfortunately, they do not. The transit companies fail to take advantage of the nature of their demand, and in so doing, contribute to their dismal revenue situation. . . .

The single-fare system is not an accident. Such a fare system has an advantage—an advantage that transit companies have been loath to lose—ease of collection. Once the single fare is paid, riders require no further surveillance. No tickets are sold, and no checking is neccessary to see that the passengers go only a prescribed distance. These savings in simplicity and in tickey-policing manpower can be considerable. . . .

Granted this, however, even where the transit companies can easily differentiate fares, they rarely have done so. It is noteworthy that no United States city having both rail and bus transit has a base fare differential of more than a nickel between types of service, even though rail transit service is generally faster than bus and the average trip length is much greater. Base fare differentials and more than nominal transfer charges between buses and rapid transit are obvious places for rationalizing the pricing system. But even this has not been done.

At this point in the era of automation, the problem of expensive labor for collecting fares really becomes academic. The technology for automatic fare collection is now so easily available and relatively so cheap, that there is no need for human fare collection or direct ticket surveillance at either end of the trip. . . .

MASS TRANSPORTATION: FUTURE IN THE PRESENT. Altogether, the serious problems of our big city mass transportation systems are soluble. The economic demands for service exist, and with proper attention given to pricing, comfort, etc., the mass transportation industry will begin to do its job in a manner befitting economic enterprise in the latter part of the twentieth century. This holds true for both rapid transit systems and commuter railroads.

In many places, the stirrings of a new mass transportation future are already being seen. In San Francisco, in particular, there is real attention being paid to the things that matter in mass transit. In the Bay Area Rapid Transit District, the new service will be frequent and fast. The cars will be clean, modern, and comfortable with no standees. The fare will vary appropriately according to distance. There will automatic fare collection machinery. Transit vehicles will be automated. All these features will contribute to making a system that should be a prototype for twentieth century transit.

In other cities, too, the changes are beginning. In Boston, a much larger system is getting out of the planning stages, and the present system is being substantially upgraded through new equipment and long overdue renovation and modernization of stations. In certain stations it is now a pleasure rather than an obscene pain to enter the Boston subway. In Chicago, more transit lines are being built, and the new equipment there is comfortable, smooth riding, and air-conditioned. Cleveland and Philadelphia are also building new lines and buying new equipment. Other cities are in varying stages of designing completely new transit systems. Even New York, the king of transit and of transit problems, is advancing. There, too, new equipment is slowly spreading through the system. Different types of communications for better service and safety are being tested and adopted. New lines are being built. All over, the transformation in transit is beginning to get under way. . . .

THE GOVERNMENT IN MASS TRANSPORTATION. There is no question that the Federal Government plays an increasingly large role in furthering the changes in mass transportation. Many of the improvements that show that mass transportation can be good business are financed, in part, by Federal demonstration and other grants. Much of present-day mass transportation research is financed, directly or indirectly by the Federal Government. . . .

The whole mechanization and automation revolution that has transformed vast sectors of our economy has just begun to touch mass transportation. And mass transportation is an ideal place for it. The moving of large numbers of people has enormous potential for being a much more capital intensive business. Typical transit companies now spend about 70 per cent of their budget for labor. This can and should drop dramatically. The returns to investment in mass transportation technology research and development are very high.

Unfortunately, the ability of individual firms to underwrite the necessary expenditures is limited. No mass transportation company alone has the resource to undertake the development and testing of new technologies that individually may or may not work out. Prototypes of new—and often good—systems tend to be very expensive. For this reason, Government intervention through sponsored research and demonstration grants is enlightened and rewarding social policy. . . .

A further point should be considered. There is a substantial amount of causal evidence to support the popular contention that mass transportation management, both transit and commuter rail, is conservative, old-fashioned, and extremely resistant to change. To the extent that this is true, regardless of who is to blame, the infusion of Federal monies into the industry must certainly be a salutary development. If nothing else, Federal aid to mass transportation will hasten the day when the owners of mass transportation capital realize the economic potential of their property. When this happens, they will no longer believe that the results of poor management can be tolerated, and they will end such management. When that time comes, the transformation of mass transportation will have come of age: the forces causing it will be self-sustaining and irresistible.

11 ═══════════

═══════════ The Bay Area
Rapid Transit
System

With the turn of public opinion toward modern new transit systems, San
Francisco's Bay Area Rapid Transit received close study by transportation experts from around the nation. BART officials were attempting to establish the
first completely new transit system in an American city in fifty years, and they
sought to do so by tapping the most recent electronic and engineering
concepts. As could readily have been anticipated, BART encountered many
setbacks and problems. One of the most critical was rapidly rising costs, a
backwash of the inflationary pressures of the late sixties and the seventies. Of
course, the failure of the federal government to provide significant levels of
funding for transit systems meant that BART had to rely almost totally upon
local sources for its multimillion dollar program. Lest the reader become too
ecstatic about the future of urban mass transit in the United States, the
following press release by BART in the autumn of 1973 gives one pause for
serious reflection.

Document†

A potential gap between revenues and costs ranging from $10 million in
the 73/74 fiscal year $27 million in 1977-78 was reported to BART's
Administration Committee Tuesday (Sept. 18).

BART staff members told the committee that prime factors in the
increased costs were impact of the three-year labor settlement; deferral of full
revenue service into San Francisco; higher than anticipated maintenance costs,
and the probability of an annual deficit for express bus service.

Short-run remedies were recommended to the directors which, if adopted,
would finance most of the deficit in the next two years.

In the longer run, the report points up the need for additional tax support,
possibly combined with a fare increase.

BART staff members emphasized that they are not advocating a fare
increase now, but made it clear that such an increase would be needed soon
unless other revenue sources are developed.

William F. Goelz, BART's Director of Finance, told directors: "Closing
the gap between revenues and costs brings into focus some critical public
policy dicisions for BART and the Bay Area." He added that in 1957 the
State Legislature decided BART must pay most of its operating costs out of

---

†From: Bay Area Rapid Transit District, Press Release, September 17, 1973.

the fare box. "It is now 1973 and it is appropriate that this policy decision be re-examined," Goelz said.

Directors were told that a country-wide awakening to the need for mass transportation was focused on the Bay Area, as well as on the problems inherent in financing such service.

Goelz said: "We are now faced with the prospect of raising fares and curtailing services in an effort—perhaps futile—to bring our costs and revenues into line, or with seeking changes in policy with regard to BART subsidies."

Other sources of funding examined by the BART staff included property, sales and personal income taxes, as well as bridge tolls, gasoline and automobile taxes.

For example, a sales tax of 0.124% would raise $10 million yearly, while a 0.31% sales tax would raise $25 million.

It was pointed out that a 25% BART fare increase could produce as much as $7 million more in revenue per year, and that a 75¢ parking charge might raise as much as $1 million yearly.

On the other hand, the Administration Committee was told, such a move would reduce BART ridership by millions of trips per year, and that most of the lost patronage would revert to the automobile. Cost for providing for those extra automobile trips likely would be far greater than the subsidy required for mass transit, the staff reported.

Directors were told that the recently-adopted MTC Plan indicates a need for more—not less—transit travel, and the BART staff stressed that therefore it indicated the District's need to address the larger question of the proper mix of revenues and subsidies to support BART. The staff added that another MTC report showed that *all* transit operators in the Bay Area are facing growing financial difficulties, and that BART was drawing attention to its own problems by putting them into a five-year context.

Goelz summed up the report by stating: "Because of the regional requirement for increased transit operating expenses and because of the regional concerns for improved reliance on transit, the policy issue of how much tax support and how much fare support should be addressed in the context of MTC's transportation plan. However, BART has no alternative sources of funds to meet our projected deficit, and is forced to assume a leadership role in gaining those funds."

12

A Balanced Transportation System

The question of alternative systems of urban transportation received discussion as the United States moved into the 1970's. By that time even such well-known friends of the highway as Secretary of Transportation John Volpe were now moving toward a reassessment of the impact of the urban freeway system. The phrase, "balanced transportation system," became a new buzz word among transportation planners. The crucial role of the Trust Fund figured prominently in these discussions because of the self-perpetuation system that produced ever more highways each year. It perhaps is ironic that the Nixon administration would be the one to reorient the nation's urban transportation system away from an almost total reliance upon the automobile and the expressway, because it was Mr. Nixon himself, as vice-president in 1954, who presented the grand highway plan of the Eisenhower administration to the Governors' Conference at Bolton Landing, New York. Typical of the search for alternatives during the early 1970's is the following essay by Ken Kelley and Richard Herbert of the Insurance Institute for Highway Safety.

Document†

Road building's longstanding trust-fund arrangement with Congress is on its way out, and in its stead a general transportation trust fund hovers on the legislative horizon.

Fifteen years ago Congress enacted the highway trust fund and the Interstate Highway program, and the United States confidently embarked on its expressway era, convinced that it could defend itself against the imminent chaos of surface transportation by pouring a Maginot Line of high-speed roads in, around and between its cities.

Today, when the 42.500-mile network of expressways is almost completed, the nation's transportation debilities are even more severe than they were in 1956—particularly in and near the highway-linked cities themselves. The nation's faith that freeways and cars could meet its transportation pressure has been painfully shattered.

Mayors, Congressional leaders and even such old-shoe allies of the road builders as governors are rebelling against the highway program's hammerlock on "highway use" taxes. The House and Senate Public Works Committees,

†From: Ken Kelley and Richard Herbert, "Priorities or Trust Funds?" *The Nation*, April 19, 1971, pp. 497-500.

historically friendly to highway spending, declined in the last session of Congress to approve the full-scale extension of the program through 1985 that was sought by road lobbyists. Instead, they set, and the Congress approved, a 1977-cutoff date, pending a "needs estimate" for the period 1976-90 that must be developed by the Department of Transportation and sent to Congress this year.

When the bulldozers and graders started to penetrate densely populated urban centers in the mid-1960s, popular support for the program began to wither. Public anger at road-building abuses has by now pulled highway officials and their programs down from a position of unquestioned domination over national surface transportation policy to one of growing accountability to increasingly harsh questioning of highway-planning practices and spending priorities. The highway trust fund has become a symbol of all that has gone wrong in the expressway era.

Eager to dissociate themselves from the highway fund's sagging reputation, road interest groups are themselves beginning to speak favorably about a general transportation trust fund. They would like it to include a sheltered account that sets highway-generated taxes aside for spending on highway projects only—sort of a fund-within-a-fund—but as the highway fund's expiration date draws closer, the road lobbyists are likely to drop this unrealistic projectionist demand. They will reason that it's better to have the security of some kind of earmarked federal money that must be shared with others—than none at all. In terms of industry self-interest, they will be right. That an earmarked fund will best serve public policy is another matter to be considered in a moment.

Already, the White House has proposed, as part of its long-term revenue-sharing push, a special kitty made up of some $2 billion drawn annually from federal airway and highway trust funds and the general treasury. This new fund would be parceled out to state and local governments, which could use their shares on whatever sorts of transportation projects they saw fit. A weakness of the proposal is that $4 billion a year in Interstate funds would still remain in the highway trust fund, exempt from local discretionary use.

Meanwhile, a general transportation trust fund idea has been pushed, gently but seriously, by Transportation Secretary John Volpe, who has said more than once that he agrees "in principle" to the eventual reformation of the road fund into an all-purpose depository that could gather tax revenues from non-highway as well as highway use—the latter, though, would far outweigh all other sources combined—and might also be supplemented with donations from the general treasury. (Highway use tax revenues now in the highway trust fund may be used only for road building, and 80 per cent of the $5 billion-a-year account goes to interstate mileage.)

Volpe is not risking his or the Administration's political necks; the electorate is becoming so disenchanted with highway projects and highway people that even the most rabid road boosters in Congress think twice these days before speaking out on behalf of road builders. One who did not think twice was George Fallon, long-time chairman of the House Public Works Committee, which has jurisdiction over highway bills. Fallon's persistent, unabashed flying of the road lobby's standard contributed to his primary defeat last fall in Baltimore—a city still smarting from the effects of heavy-handed expressway planning that fell particularly harshly on black residents.

The idea of a transportation trust fund has bipartisan support in both houses of Congress, and last summer the National Governors' Conference, once a champion of the highway trust fund, jolted the road lobby by demanding that the federal government so amend its laws that each governor might "exercise his executive prerogatives ... by having the ability to transfer, upon a limited basis, funds among the various federal transportation trust funds and grant programs to meet his own state's priority transportation needs." In other words, governors now want the right to spend federal highway trust fund dollars on non-highway transportation improvements—mass-transit development, intercity rail service, conceivably even air terminal or seaport modernization.

It is a right that more and more governors are exercising over state highway trust funds. State legislators have begun lifting the ban against using state-raised gasoline taxes for purposes other than road expansion and maintenance. Maryland, at the behest of Gov. Marvin Mandel, created both a state department of transportation *and* a truly intermodal transportation improvement fund, although to get his proposals through, Mandel had to withstand a singularly abusive, emotion-pitched campaign of opposition by the American Automobile Association and allied road-support organizations. Twelve other states now have intermodal transportation departments, a few of which have the right to "divert" state gasoline taxes to nonhighway projects. At least eight other states are considering such departments.

Many mayors were trying to supplant the federal highways-or-nothing fund with a general transportation fund well before Volpe and other federal policy makers took up the cause. As the elected official who often stood helplessly by while his city was disfigured and dismembered by unwanted freeways forced upon it by federal and state policies, the mayor learned early in the Interstate program that roadway blessings could be mixed indeed. In most states, highway decisions have been openly handed down or covertly engineered by the state highway agency and the governor. Unless he was particularly tough-minded, the mayor found himself rubber-stamping whatever state road planners and federal policies had determined to do to his community.

And when he did resist, the cost could be high. San Francisco's Mayor John Shelly could not have taken much pleasure from rejecting nearly $300 million in federal assistance in 1966; but reject it he did, because the money could be used only for building expressway mileage that the city's inhabitants neither wanted nor needed. Mayor John Lindsay of New York was faced more recently with the same sorry choice when he turned down the Cross-Brooklyn and Lower Manhattan expressways—two road-building schemes that are anathema to New Yorkers but to which would have been attached many tens of millions of trust-fund dollars.

Such sacrifices of federal road dollars—money collected from urban as well as rural drivers—are especially galling to cities because they have desperately needed, but have usually been unable to get, similarly large sums of federal-aid money to develop or improve downtown and suburban mass-transportation systems, and thus tempt the public away from cars and into alternate, congestion-relieving means of peak-hour travel. The car-owning city dweller's contribution to the trust fund, made via gas taxes, has simply bought him a bigger transportation headache. . . .

It makes no public policy sense to project the concept of the highway trust fund into the broadened frame of general transportation. The highway fund generated abuses, and there is no reason to assume that an intermodal fund could avoid the same evils. Even a well-conceived transportation trust fund could develop some of the highway trust fund's worst features: insulation from periodic review and adjustment, growth unrelated to public need, and propagation of outsized lobbies.

Earmarked money circumvents the traditional budget and review processes of government. What determines the size and growth rate of earmarked funds is not public need but the amount of revenue produced by statutorily committed taxes—in the case of the highway fund, gasoline and other "highway use" taxes that swell in volume as more people drive more cars that use more gasoline on more new highways.

James Nelson, an Amherst College professor who specializes in transportation problems, warned the Senate Subcommittee on Economy in Government in 1969 that when Congress invests the public's money on such terms it sacrifices "policy planning, economic analysis and Congressional scrutiny," and requires instead "a total level of federal expenditure" based on the fund's income "rather than the prospective demand which should be efficiently met."

In the case of road building financed by the trust fund, spending has not only failed to reflect accurately the level of public demand for highways as opposed to other modes of transportation; it has also ignored the proper place of highways in the ranking of all national priorities. Schools, housing, urban redevelopment, pollution abatement, health care, police protection and job training contend in the open market for public money; road building, assigned to a trust fund, does not.

Furthermore, a trust fund tends to breed a sprawling complex of economic interests, which can be counted on to warn of economic dislocation, real or imagined, when the fund shrinks or disappears. A complete list of the highway trust fund's "welfare recipients" would fill pages. It would include 5,500 member companies of the American Road Builders Association; "highway construction provides their only income," ARBA says. It would also include those who sell and make cars, on whose behalf the president of the Automobile Manufacturers Association proclaimed in 1955 that adoption of the Interstate program would help market "a net gain of 23 million vehicles in use by 1965." (His prophecy was close to the mark: during the trust fund's first nine years—from July 1, 1956 to July 1, 1965—motor vehicle registration swelled by 22.7 million vehicles.) It would include also the companies belonging to the Portland Cement Association Asphalt Institute, American Trucking Associations, National Association of Motor Bus Owners and—the misnomered star atop the crown of the highway movement—the Highway Users Federation for Safety and Mobility. It would include, finally, the millions of workers who pay dues to the Teamsters, United Auto Workers and various highway construction trade unions. Transforming the highway trust fund into a transportation trust fund might well serve to escalate the inflexible highway lobby into a bigger, but still inflexible, transportation lobby in which pavers, materials makers, vehicle manufacturers and various industrial and union relatives put aside their healthy differences in order to protect an expanded source of guaranteed dollars from public tampering and periodic Congressional adjustment.

There is also the danger that when government adopts a trust-funding policy it commits itself to alliance with the industry for which perpetuation of the fund becomes an end in itself. The highway lobby now consists of more than the contractors who build roads and the industrialists who refine oil and make cars; it also includes state highway officials, U.S. Government administrators of highway munificence and political horse traders of freeway projects in federal and state legislatures.

In addition to the lessons offered by the highway trust fund, the Transportation Department and Congress have had a recent opportunity to observe how a method different from the transportation fund might work. Harassed by mounting urban pressures for a decently funded federal aid-to-mass-transit program, Volpe announced in early 1969 that he favored using auto excise taxes for a mass-transit trust fund. Despite auto industry opposition, he asked the White House to include a mass-transit trust fund in the Administration's levislative program. The Bureau of the Budget, long-time unsuccessful foe of the highway trust fund, balked; so instead of a trust fund, the White House agreed that mass transit should seek "contract authority"—funds from the general treasury set aside by Congress in advance for specified long-term programs. Doomed to go away empty-handed if they held out for a trust fund, the transit men resigned themselves to supporting the Administration's approach.

Mass-transit lobbyists—equipment makers, bus owners, and organized urban and public-transit officials—then effected a resourceful stratagem: they moved to enlist their traditional enemies, the highway advocates, to their cause. They reasoned that if highway devotees wanted to make sure that mass transit would not some day attempt to raid the highway trust fund—as it tried, without result, in the mid-1960s—or to get control of auto excise taxes, they ought to join in the lobbying effort to endow mass transit with its own long-term financial guarantee from the federal government.

While highway supporters did not rush to testify in favor of mass transit's program, their earlier opposition was silenced and a few components of the powerful highway lobby—most notably the Automobile Manufacturers Association—did actually show up to testify to the "urgent need" for urban public transportation assistance.

Most highway lobbyists took advantage of the new issue to promote their own cause as well—preservation of the highway trust fund in its undiluted form. A typical highway lobby statement on behalf of the transit program was presented by Lyman W. Slack, president of the National Automobile Dealers Association, to the Senate Subcommittee on Housing and Urban Affairs. In a curious twist of logic, Slack said that government should not break its "contractual and trust relationship" with highway users that guarantees their taxes will be used for highways only, but that while "one does not have to look very far" to see the need for improved public transportation, *its* funding should come from the general treasury so that "Congress will be in a flexible position [and] not be limited to specified sources of revenue."

The freeway-subway marriage of convenience worked well. In October 1970, President Nixon signed into law a "contract authority" act passed in substantially the form he had proposed in August 1969: a twelve-year program to spend an intended $10 billion. The Transportation Department can now enter into contracts with local transit governing agencies that guarantees them a schedule of matching grants extending over a five-year period, even though Congress has not yet appropriated the funds. The law sets limits on the amounts that can be scheduled for paying out in grants each year to the local agencies, and limits to $3.1 billion the amount the department can obligate during the first five years. The Congress has committed itself to appropriate in future years the amounts of money needed to make good on the grants, within the limits set by Congress. Thus a local transit agency has the assurance—once it enters into a contract with the department—of continued federal funding; it will not be left with an empty hole in the ground once it has started a project.

A mass-transit trust fund would have been pegged on earmarked tax sources. The "contract authority" is not. Its money will be appropriated out of the general treasury. The transportation secretary must report to Congress every two years the amount he thinks he will need to obligate for two years beyond his current authorizations—thus always maintaining a five-years-in-advance program of contracts with local agencies. In this way, Congress can expand or whittle the transit program's authorizations every two years, basing its decisions on shifts in national spending priorities.

With the new federal program, the entire field of urban mass transit is expected to explode into a turmoil of buying and selling. Supply firms such as General Electric, Westinghouse, Rohr Corporation (makers of San Francisco's BART cars), Pullman-Standard, St. Louis Car, General Signal and Westinghouse Air Brake will undoubtedly take advantage of the new market by throwing more and more resources into their transit system divisions—and those divisions can be relied on in the future to wail quite as loudly about economic hardship over any proposal to cut back their federal financing as do highway interests today.

If national priorities eventually were to shift away from urban transit, such companies and the government agencies to which they sell—both at the urban level and in the DOT—would try to keep the transit assistance pump running at peak capacity. But a safeguard is available in urban mass transit's "contract authority," which anticipates that Congress will control the aid program through its biennial authorizations process.

A general transportation trust fund may seem to the Transportation Department to be an obvious outgrowth of the highway trust fund, but if there had never been a highway trust fund, and if road construction were being paid for today, like everything else, out of the general treasury on the basis of contract authority and periodic review, no responsible federal official would consider paying for transportation projects in any way different. Contract authority may yet be the best approach to a viable long-term transportation improvement policy.

Under contract authority, an overdue measure of flexibility could be introduced into overall transportation priority setting. Determination of which major transportation projects are to be funded out of an omnibus "transportation contract authority" could be left largely to local communities. Taxes would no longer be assigned "use" labels but would become transportation resources which, if unused, would revert to the general treasury. Meanwhile, lesser spot improvements of transportation facilities—those not requiring long-term financing—would vie for resources from the general treasury just as other public programs do. Thus, once again, a project would have reasonable assurance of being carried through to completion, but would not have the particularly onerous aftereffect of leaving a purse of unused, accumulating federal dollars going in search of other projects.

All this would require a restructuring of the administrative machinery that now runs transport spending programs—a restructuring, as the Kennedy-Koch bill puts it, to "assure effective, coordinated policy management cutting across rigid modal lines." As organized at present, the Transportation Department is a holding company for a half dozen semi-autonomous bureaucracies, each jealous of its realm and assigned dollars. If transportation is to become truly balanced, then the department must become a single agency in fact as well as name, able to fit solutions to problems instead of simply fitting programs to money, political muscle or policy inertia.

13

Richard Nixon's Address on "Transportation Initiatives," 1974

The sudden energy crisis that struck the United States in late 1973 stimulated sudden interest in urban transit. The rapidity with which the Nixon administration responded to the long-demonstrated need for better balance in the nation's transportation system surprised most knowledgeable observers. On February 9, 1974, the president put forth a bold program in a special nationwide radio broadcast. The following week he sent to Capitol Hill a detailed legislative proposal that included the outlay of $19 billion by 1977. His leadership received widespread support, even during the travails of Watergate, and virtually no serious objections were raised, although as usual many particulars received critical comment. And, if Congress would support the president's request, then perhaps the financial difficulties that plagued BART could be solved.

Document†
Good afternoon.

From the earliest days of your history, transportation has played a vital role in the progress of America. Clipper ships, canal boats, toll roads and railroads fed the American economy, linked communities across our expanding Nation, and joined our Nation with the world. Mass production of the automobile, linked with the most advanced highway system in the world, has made us a nation on wheels.

We have the largest and most diverse transportation system in the world today. As our society shifts and grows, and as our economy expands, we must ensure that the effectiveness of this system keeps pace with the changing demands placed upon it. In the past five years, we have made great forward strides in this effort.

We have completed major sections of the Interstate Highway System.

The Airport and Airway Development Act, passed in 1970, has provided significant new Federal financial assistance to our Nation's airports.

†From: Richard M. Nixon, "Nationwide Radio Address on Transportation Initiatives for the Nation," February 9, 1974.

We have established a successful program aimed at eliminating air piracy.

We have acted to bring about dramatic reductions in transportation accident and fatility rates.

We have created AMTRAK, a new corporation to improve passenger service on the Nation's railways, and last year there was a 14 percent increase in rail passengers.

We have increased Federal aid to urban public transportation to $1 billion a year—that is eight times the level of 1968—through the Urban Mass Transportation Act.

The Merchant Marine Act of 1970 marked the most comprehensive change in our approach to the problems of the U.S. flag merchant marines in almost 35 years.

Through the Federal-Aid Highway Act of 1973, we are permitting States and localities to use a portion of their Federal highway funds for public transit.

The Regional Rail Reorganization Act of 1973 will permit a needed restructuring of the bankrupt railroads of the Northeast and Midwest into a streamlined, privately owned system.

While we have made encouraging progress, the job is not completed. These are some of our goals ahead:

We have to find ways to use our enormous transportation systems in a more flexible manner. In many cases, these systems, such as our subways and our urban highways, are utilized at maximum capacity for two or three hours during the day, and scarcely at all in the remainder of the day.

In the past ten years, we have become increasingly conscious of the effects of our transportation systems on our environment. We must now give equal attention to the need for energy conservation as we design and utilize these transportation systems.

And finally, Federal regulation has served to restrict the growth of some of our systems at the expense of others, with the result that we do not have sufficient balance in the choice of transportation available to us.

Our efforts must continue to concentrate on achieving the goals of flexibility in the use of our transportation systems, economy in the use of our energy resources and balance in the availability of diverse forms of transportation.

To achieve these goals in the areas of urban and rural public transportation, I will send to the Congress next week a Unified Transportation Assistance Program. This program would authorize $16 billion in Federal assistance for metropolitan and rural transportation over the next six years. Two-thirds of this amount would be allocated to State and local Governments for application in areas where they believe this money can be spent most effectively.

Local officials, who understand your community better than anybody here in Washington, would determine transportation priorities, choosing between construction of highways or public transit systems, or the purchase of buses or rail cars. This would provide for flexibility between capital investments and other expenses.

The Unified Transportation Assistance Program will mark the largest Federal commitment ever to the improvement of public transportation in our cities and towns. Its objective is to provide you with diverse forms of public transportation that take into account the need for transportation without environmental damage, without wasted energy, and, if possible, without congestion.

Let me turn now from the problem of transportation within our cities to the problem of transportation between our cities.

A healthy rail system is essential to the development of a balanced transportation system.

Nothing has hindered the economic health of our Nation's rail systems more than the outmoded and complex Federal regulations which govern those systems. These regulations have prevented the railroads from maintaining a competitive position with other forms of transportation.

The collapse of the Penn Central Railroad is ample evidence of the wrongheadedness of this approach. While we cannot afford to let our railroads fail, neither can be afford to bail them out every time they get in trouble. Our economy cannot afford it, and our taxpayers will not tolerate it.

If we are to revitalize our railroads, we must shift the focus of our concern from outmoded rules to economic realities. We cannot meet jet-age transportation requirements with horse and buggy regulations.

The inability of our railroads to compete with other forms of transportation has seriously affected this vital industry. The railroads often cannot afford to make necessary improvements in tracks, terminals and equipment. The result has been a steady deterioration of service.

To modernize and revitalize our system of rail transportation, I will submit to the Congress next week the Transportation Improvement Act of 1974. This act is aimed at restoring this Nation's railroads to their proper place in the national transportation system.

The proposal would authorize $2 billion in Federal loan guarantees to help railroads invest in their tracks, their terminals and their equipment. These loan guarantees are not a signal that we intend to provide public handouts to our railroads. They are, on the contrary, intended to restore the railroads to a position in which they can once again compete economically with other methods of transportation, and thereby support themselves without Federal assistance.

But this cannot happen until we adjust the Federal regulations which created the problem in the first place. Therefore, the Transportation Improvement Act would significantly overhaul Federal regulations governing rail freight carriers. In addition, it would eliminate the practice of discrimination through taxation which has further contributed to the economic problems of our railroads.

One of the most significant moments in our history occurred in 1769 when the Union Pacific Railroad, building west from Omaha, met the Central Pacific, building east from Sacramento. The joining of our Nation in this manner opened a whole new era of economic growth for America. Today our railroads are more necessary than ever. They make extremely efficient use of fuel with little negative effect on the environment and they deliver nearly 35 percent of the Nation's freight at low cost. The essential tracks are there, the system that crisscrosses the country with a web of steel rails is in place. Now we must make it work again.

As we act to improve our urban and rural transportation and to restore our national rail system, we must not neglect those parts of our national transportation system that have proved successful.

And chief among these is our highway system, which is among the very best in the world.

Today the Interstate Highway System stretches from the Atlantic to the Pacific. By the early 1980's, when completed, this system will carry over 20 percent of all highway traffic.

Our programs for highway safety are continually being improved, and funding for State and community highway safety programs will be increased, both to encourage State enactment of mandatory seatbelt legislation and to get the drunk driver off the road. . . .

Today, more than ever, the quality of American life and the growth of our economy is dependent upon our ability to move people and goods rapidly, safely, comfortably and efficiently.

The programs that I have outlined for you this afternoon are designed to ensure that America's transportation system keeps pace with our needs.

Thank you and good afternoon.

14

The Impact of
Mass Transit

The program presented to Congress in 1974 by the Nixon administration constituted in large part a repackaging of existing monies. Yet, as the following assessment by the *Christian Science Monitor* points out, finally large sums would be poured into urban transit. Although the fate of the Nixon program was unknown at the time of the completion of this book, it appeared that the Nixon program would receive congressional approval in some form that followed fairly closely along the lines of the president's suggestion. Unlike the situation in 1956, when Congress passed the Interstate program, everyone now recognized that this legislation would have a critical impact upon urban America for years to come. Thus this editorial, typical of those that appeared in the wake of the president's message, coupled enthusiasm with a cautious and tentative attitude. The editors knew full well the enormous problem that confronted urban America.

Document†
President Nixon sent to Congress a $16 billion, six-year mass transit bill. It reflects a welcome awakening commitment to mass transit by the administration—albeit at the prompting of the energy crisis.

It should be noted that the $16 billion, or about $2.5 billion a year, is not all new money. More than a billion dollars each year, for example, is urban transportation money now being spent under the Highway Act. Perhaps a fourth of the $16 billion, if Congress approves the proposal, would be newly allocated.

Also, the proposal should be viewed in terms of what level of spending is necessary. The American Transit Association has been calling for $2.5 billion a year in federal aid for capital spending alone, plus another $1 billion a year for the next two years for "emergency" aid, including relief for operating deficits of local transit systems. This would mean outlays of $3.5 billion per year, a billion more than the President's request.

The case for greater mass transit spending has been easier to see for many Americans while they have sat in long lines waiting to fill their tanks with gasoline. But as we have earlier warned in these columns, the case for mass transit should not be so closely tied to the inconvenience of the moment that enthusiasm for it might wane with the availability of more gasoline. The ATA is correct in calling for the development of a farsighted national

†From: "Money for Mass Transit." Reprinted by permission from *The Christian Science Monitor,* February 11, 1974. © 1974 The Christian Science Publishing Society. All rights reserved.

transportation policy, with federal leadership and coordination. The administration, however, appears to want to stay on the underside of the range of possible mass transit efforts.

The administration, with an echo of its revenue sharing proposals, proposes that part of the federal mass transit money be spent at the discretion of local leaders for buses or rail transit—or, conceivably, and to the horror of mass transit supporters, for roads.

Congress should look at the administration's proposals as a base-line target for its mass transit decisions. Just in terms of new rider loads on existing transit systems, greater funds are needed to offset higher deficits. A 50 percent larger bus fleet is called for.

The United States continues to spend some $20 billion a year on highways. Hundreds of billions of dollars will be invested by the oil industry in the next decade to fuel the automobile fleet on the highways. Next to these outlays, even the proposed new level of investment in mass transit seems low.

Government policy in such areas is crucial. The growth of the second most populous urban region in America, Los Angeles, during the car age finds 88.8 percent of workers dependent on the auto to get to work. But in New York, the most populous urban area with a transit system developed before the huge federal push for the auto, only 50 percent of the workers must drive to work.

Congress's mass transit decision on the White House proposal will help mold the lifestyle of America for decades to come.

part three

Bibliographic Essay

It is regrettable that historians have not devoted much attention to the role of the automobile and the highway in American life. As the preceding material has pointed out, both have played an important role in the history of the United States during the twentieth century. Those students seeking to go beyond the material contained in this volume will necessarily have to go to the specialized journals of transportation experts and government reports. The technical literature of the subject of highways is extraordinarily large, and no brief bibliography such as this can do more than touch upon the major available sources. Consequently, except for a few articles of major importance, this review will be restricted to published books. However, students might consult especially *American City; Power Wagon, The Motor Truck Journal; Traffic Engineering; Roads and Streets; American Highways; Journal of the American Institute of Planners; Architectural Forum;* and *Civil Engineering.*

There are several excellent general works that will provide the student with a useful overview. The best place to start is with John Rae, *The Road and the Car in American Life* (Boston, 1971). Rae's book is based upon the assumption that the automobile has been one of the most important positive developments in the nation's history, and he describes the manner in which federal and state highway policies have served the needs of the automobile. Perhaps equally important is Sam Bass Warner's intriguing and suggestive *The Urban Wilderness* (New York, 1972); Warner places the role of the automobile and highway into a much larger urban frame of reference; but his study is indispensable for the serious student of American urban history. So also is the iconoclastic and penetrating analysis of the "urban crisis" by the distinguished Harvard political scientist, Edward C. Banfield. His *The Unheavenly City* (Boston, 1970) is required reading for anyone concerned with life in our modern cities. Several other books will provide the student with the necessary perspective from within to understand the role of the automobile and the expressway: For starters, try James Q. Wilson, ed., *The Metropolitan Enigma; Inquiries into the Nature and Dimensions of America's "Urban Crisis"* (Boston, 1968), and Daniel P. Moynihan, *Toward a National Urban Policy* (New York, 1970).

Several standard volumes upon the history of American urban development will also be useful. See especially, Charles N. Glaab and A. Theodore Brown, *A History of Urban America* (New York, 1967); it is especially good for the period between 1815 and 1920. Blake McKelvey's two volume series is also useful: see *The Urbanization of America, 1860-1915*, and *The Emergence of Metropolitan America, 1915-1966* (New Brunswick, 1963, 1968).

The best place to start in a study of American highway policy and the automobile is John Rae, *The Road and the Car in American Life* (Boston, 1971). His standard interpretation emphasizes the positive nature of both the automobile and the highway policy pursued by the federal government. Several other studies are also of utility: John B. Rae, *The American Automobile: A Brief History* (Chicago, 1965); James J. Flink, *America Adopts the Automobile, 1895-1910* (New York, 1970); Blaine Brownell, "A Symbol of Modernity; Attitudes Toward the Automobile in Southern Cities in the 1920s," *American Quarterly*, March, 1972, pp. 20-44; James J. Flink, "Three States of American Automobile Consciousness," *American Quarterly*, October, 1972, pp. 451-73. For a different perspective, see Allan Nevins's useful biography of Henry Ford, *Ford: The Times, The Man, The Company* (New York, 1954). See also, the Automobile Manufacturers, *Automobiles in America* (Detroit, 1962).

The standard study of highway policy is Rae, *The Road and the Car in American Life,* but the excellent doctoral dissertation by Mark H. Rose,

Express Highway Politics, 1939-1956 (Ph.D. dissertation, Ohio State University, 1973), should be consulted. However, the real history can best be found in the myriad of government publications, especially the annual reports of the Bureau of Public Roads. See also, *A Story of the Beginning, Purpose, Growth, Activities, and Achievements of AASHO* (Washington, D.C., 1964) for a favorable series of activities about highway construction in the United States by executives of the American Association of State Highway Officials. Of special interest to this study is the Clay Committee Report, *A Ten-Year National Highway Program; A Report to the President* (January 1955). Much of the detail regarding the Eisenhower administration's deliberations is based upon manuscript sources located in the Dwight D. Eisenhower Library, Abilene, Kansas. However, these materials merely supplement the printed public record at the time, although the issue of toll roads seems to have been more divisive within the administrative circles than reported in the press. The standard studies of the Eisenhower administration do not contribute anything to our understanding of highway policy, but they do provide an understanding of the temper of the times and the thinking of the administrative leaders that is essential for understanding the political climate that produced the Interstate system. See Eisenhower's ponderous memoirs, *Mandate for Change, 1953-1956* (New York, 1963), and *Waging Peace, 1956-1961,* (New York, 1965). For a critical evaluation, see Emmet Hughes, *Ordeal of Power* (New York, 1963) and Robert J. Donovan, *Eisenhower: The Inside Story* (New York, 1956).

The literature on urban planning is often overlooked by students of history, but one ignores this important aspect of the picture at his own peril. The standard work is Mel Scott, *American City Planning Since 1890* (Berkeley, 1969), but it should be supplemented by Christopher Tunnard and Henry Reed *American Skyline* (New York, 1955). Warner's *Urban Wilderness* provides many new insights into the planning process, and Roy Lubove's *Twentieth-Century Pittsburgh* (New York, 1969) is an excellent case study. See also Alan Altschuler, *The City Planning Process* (Ithaca, 1956), while Norman J. Johnston's unpublished doctoral dissertation, "Harland Bartholomew: His Comprehensive Plans and Science of Planning," (University of Pennsylvania, 1964), provides a useful study of this pioneering city planner. Also useful is Jeanne R. Lowe, *Cities in a Race for Time* (New York, 1967).

The literature on the impact of the automobile upon urban areas is rich and diverse, although there is no single volume that provides a comprehensive study. Students could easily start with Edward Banfield's *Unheavenly City* and Warner's *Urban Wilderness.* Of particular value are three books by Wilfred Owen, *The Accessible City* (Washington, D.C. 1972); *Cities in the Motor Age* (New York, 1959); and *The Metropolitan Transportation Problem* (Washington, D.C. 1956). Lewis Mumford, *The Urban Prospect* (New York, 1968) not only contains his powerful essay first published in 1956 at the time of the passage of the Interstate program, but when read in conjunction with his other essays that appeared during the 1950s and 1960s, provides the reader with a broad and rich understanding of the vital relationships between urban growth and the transportation systems.

Leading an increasing number of polemical volumes extremely hostile to the freeways are: Helen Leavitt, *Superhighway—Superhoax* (New York, 1970); A. Q. Mowbray, *Road to Ruin* (Philadelphia, 1969); and John Jerome, *The Death of the Automobile* (New York, 1972). Not far behind these is Kenneth Schneider's, *Autokind vs. Mankind* (New York, 1971), a more thoughtful and incisive, yet nonetheless devastating, study. Alan Lupo et al, *Rites of Way,* (Boston, 1971) describes the struggle against the freeway in Boston. However, the reader should also consult several important magazine articles: Charlton Ogburn, Jr., "The Motorcar vs. America." *American Heritage* (June, 1970), pp. 108 ff.; Angela Rooney, "Freeways: Urban Invaders," *National Parks and Conservation Magazine* (October 1971) pp. 4 ff.; Jeremiah D. O'Leary, "Evaluating the Environmental Impact of an Urban Freeway," *Traffic Quarterly*, July, 1969, pp. 342 ff.; and Juan Cameron, "How the Interstate Changed the Face of the Nation", *Fortune*, July, 1971. See also Charles Abrams, *The Role and Responsibilities of the Federal Highway System in Baltimore* (Baltimore, 1968); Tabor Stone, *Beyond the Automobile; Reshaping the Transportation Environment* (New York, 1971); and John R. Meyer, et al, *The Urban Transportation Problem* (Cambridge, 1965).

Two major problems of modern metropolitan America are directly related to the freeway system and the overreliance upon the automobile: suburban sprawl and central city decline. The literature dealing with these important topics is massive, but students can quickly gain a sure grasp of the topics by consulting the following: Warner, *The Urban Wilderness;* Banfield, *The Unheavenly City;* Jean Gottmann, *Megalopolis: The Urbanized Northeastern Seaboard of the United States* (Cambridge, 1961); *The Exploding Metropolis,* by the editors of *Fortune,* (New York, 1958); Marion Clawson, *Suburban Land Conversion in the United States* (Baltimore, 1971); Charles Abrams, *The City is the Frontier* (New York, 1965); Daniel P. Moynihan, *Toward A National Urban Policy* (New York, 1970); Robert Fogelson, *The Fragmented Metropolis: Los Angeles, 1850-1930* (Cambridge, 1967); Benjamin Chinitz, ed., *City and Suburb: The Economics of Metropolitan Growth* (Englewood Cliffs, 1964); Scott Donaldson, *The Suburban Myth* (New York, 1969).

Most of the contemporary story of urban mass transit must be gleaned from recent periodical articles. However, consult Sam Báss Warner, *Streetcar Suburbs* (Cambridge, 1962) for an excellent study of the impact of streetcars upon Boston. Glen Holt, "The Changing Perception of Urban Pathology: An Essay on the Development of Mass Transit in the United States," in Kenneth Jackson, ed., *Cities in American History* (New York, 1972), places the question into good historical perspective. See also, George Rogers Taylor, "The Beginning of Mass Transportation in Urban America" *Smithsonian Journal of History*, Summer and Fall, 1966, pp. 35-50 and 31-54; Michael Danielson, *Federal-Metropolitan Politics and the Commuter Crisis* (New York, 1965), is useful for a perspective at the time when antifreeway sentiment had just begun to be noticed. See also, J. R. Meyer et al, *The Urban Transportation Problem* (New York, 1965).